The Trader's Journey

The Trader's Journey

Navigating the path to trading success

PETER ROBBINS

# Harriman House

HARRIMAN HOUSE LTD
Website: harriman.house

First published in 2026 by Harriman House, an imprint of Pan Macmillan
Associated companies throughout the world
www.panmacmillan.com

Copyright © Peter Robbins 2026

The right of Peter Robbins to be identified as the author has been asserted in accordance with the Copyright, Design and Patents Act 1988.

Paperback ISBN: 978-1-80409-166-1
eBook ISBN: 978-1-80409-167-8

All rights reserved. No part of this publication may be reproduced, stored in a retrieval system, or transmitted in any form or by any means (including without limitation electronic, mechanical, photocopying, recording, or otherwise) without the prior written permission of the publisher. This book is sold subject to the condition that it shall not, by way of trade or otherwise, be lent, hired out, or otherwise circulated without the publisher's prior consent. This work is reserved from text and data mining (Article 4(3) Directive (EU) 2019/790).

Harriman House does not have any control over, or any responsibility for, any author or third-party websites (including without limitation URLs, emails and QR codes) referred to in or on this book. This book is for informational purposes only. Readers are advised to consult an appropriate professional in light of their relevant circumstances and requirements before acting on any information in this book.

No responsibility or liability for loss occasioned to any person or corporate body acting or refraining to act as a result of reading material in this book can be accepted by the publisher, by the author, or by the employers of the author.

01

Printed in the United States of America.

Cover design by Paul McCarthy. Shutterstock images used.

CONTENTS

Preface	vii
Introduction: The Chosen Path	1
Chapter 1: Is Trading Really for You?	9
Chapter 2: A Trader's Education	19
Chapter 3: The Nature of the Markets	37
Chapter 4: Analytical Techniques	53
Chapter 5: Trading Styles	79
Chapter 6: Developing a Business Plan	89
Chapter 7: Developing a Detailed Trading Plan	99
Chapter 8: Examples of Trading Plans—Setups and Executions	127
Chapter 9: Trading Psychology I—Obstacles Along the Way	143
Chapter 10: Trader Psychology II—Listen to Your Heart and Trade with Your Mind	167
Conclusion	177
Recommended Reading	181
Acknowledgments	189
About the Author	191

PREFACE

I HAVE BEEN TRADING for over 50 years. I have made big money and lost big money, traded full time and traded part time, traded in the zone and traded outside the zone. No matter what, I have always traded.

Like most traders, trading is a passion for me, not a way to make a million dollars or escape the rat race. (Though, done right, it can of course achieve those things too.) It is a business that allows me to not only supplement my income but continually learn about myself—and trading.

I have learned a lot. And I love to share those lessons, helping both novices get set on the right path, as well as discussing tactics and swapping notes with experienced traders. Over the years I have met many traders and learned invaluable lessons from trading greats. I have also met a lot of people who are interested in trading. It is a privilege to show the ropes to those truly interested in learning.

I have decided to write this book to set down the lessons I most frequently share. If you are only contemplating trading or just getting started, I will help you identify if it is really for you before you begin, as well as show you how to get up and running properly. If you're already committed to trading, I will share the most important things you will encounter along the way—from opportunities to obstacles—and how to always put the odds in your favor.

If you're an experienced trader, you'll know that the only essential thing in trading is to never stop learning: and I believe this material, though written to be accessible to every experience level, will be of great value to you too. We often need to remind ourselves to keep on track. And the best tools are those that are regularly sharpened.

Let's begin.

INTRODUCTION
THE CHOSEN PATH

You've seen the ads...

"How I turned $1,000 into $10 million in two years. Anyone can become a stock market millionaire. GUARANTEED. In only ten minutes a day!"

Anyone who tries to find out about trading online can't help but be bombarded with claims of this nature. Of course, you already know they're too good to be true, or you wouldn't be here. Nothing that valuable is ever that easy. Nevertheless, finding material on how to trade these days *is* easier than ever.

The world has changed out of all recognition.

When I began trading back in the 70s, it was nearly impossible to find material on trading. There were a few classic texts on fundamental investment principles and technical analysis; material beyond this was almost nonexistent. Most trading decisions at the time were driven by fundamentals and advice from brokers. Technical trading was an obscure art form, practiced only by a fringe element, often laughed at and shunned as they manually updated their charts, drew their trend lines and strategized for the next day.

Once the personal computer came on the scene, trading took on a whole new dimension. Programs evolved that could update charts in real time and in any time frame, and include an endless number of indicators. They can be used to develop sophisticated trading systems and back test them. You can tweak them to fit your unique trading style.

There is software that you can use to run setup identification algorithms that help you sort through thousands of potential trades in seconds, alerting you to your favorite patterns and setups.

Fundamental data—formerly delayed, limited and only available in print—has been expanded to include every conceivable data set and ratio. It is updated in real time and available in multiple databases for easy access. This data can be easily filtered with multiple screening programs, to help narrow down candidates that fit any criteria you wish. Computers have taken trading to a whole new level.

At the same time, educational resources on the art of trading have multiplied beyond count. There are thousands of books on all aspects of trading. Magazines, newsletter subscriptions, blogs and tweets could keep you reading indefinitely. There are also numerous experts, some with reputations well-deserved, others merely self-proclaimed—promising riches beyond your wildest dreams.

> **Trading is easy, it's making money trading that's hard.**

You would think that, with all this technology and knowledge readily available, trading should be easy to master—certainly easier than it was in the 70s.

The reality is a little different.

Once you study trading, you soon discover that most of the material boils down to the same basic principles, which in theory will guarantee success. In fact, it is quite easy to develop trading systems that generate consistent profits. Numerous trading software programs allow users to define trading rules and parameters, back test, and produce expected results. The problem is that, when people actually try to implement the systems, things fall apart.

With all the evolution that has taken place in the world of trading, one thing hasn't changed: the statistic that approximately only 2% of commodity and 10% of stock traders succeed. Success is defined here as being able to make profits on a consistent basis over the long term. The vast majority didn't in the 70s, and they don't today.

Given that trading is basically a business of odds, you would think most people would avoid it with statistics like that. Yet something lures people in, no matter what…

After all, trading *is* simple. You buy something. If it goes up, you hold it. When it starts to go down, you sell it—hopefully at a profit. But, if not, you sell at a loss. This does not jeopardize your long-term success.

The essential rules of trading are remarkably straightforward:

- follow the trend
- cut losses short
- let winners ride
- manage your money to avoid the risk of ruin.

These are rules that work.

Why is something so simple so hard to implement successfully? That, too, is simple—though far from simple to overcome: human emotion gets in the way. When people are exposed to the opportunity to increase or lose their hard-earned capital, they misplace the ability to trade objectively. Most end up following a road to ruin.

Intellectually, we can see the rules and understand them completely. Before our money is on the line, we can grasp the consequences of breaking them. Then it's on the line. And everything changes.

The rules of trading are like a map: accurate and, from one angle, all you need to get to where you want to go. But studying a map and hiking a hundred miles are two very different things.

A journey of a thousand miles begins with a single trade.

My objective with this book is not only to cover the rules necessary for success, but also to show you how to follow them when the rubber hits the road. I will show you what it *actually* means to take the journey of a successful trader—and the consequences of your chosen path. I want to show you what it takes to stick to the path; how to follow it even in the dark, or amid the lure of shortcuts; how to overcome obstacles, and evade enemies, and persist in the face of fatigue, discouragement, and worse.

I will show you how to be in the successful minority—if you're prepared to join them. The average trader loses. Average actions destine them to failure. *The Trader's Journey* is not their path. But it can be yours.

Here's what's ahead.

THE JOURNEY TO COME

In Chapter 1, I begin by asking the question most people never ask themselves when they decide to begin trading. It's a question that, if answered honestly, could prevent a lot of pain and financial loss.

Is trading really for you?

With such a high failure rate, it follows that for most people the answer to this question is probably no. If I can help you discover this before you have lost your savings, this book will be the best investment you ever make. And if trading really *is* for you, you have nothing to lose from seriously asking this. Even experienced traders can benefit, as I'll show.

The business of trading should be pursued only by those individuals who truly understand what they are getting into. I have seen many enter the business, only to see significant amounts of capital wiped out from their accounts in no time at all. Some then leave the business, never to return. In my opinion, most should never have traded in the first place.

Others stick around, adding to their accounts. They either continue to lose over time or become better traders. In Chapter 2, I outline an education plan that will help you join the latter rather than the former group, not only laying the groundwork before you place your first trade but showing you how successful traders embrace a lifetime of learning. It is essential to stay current while trading.

The three chapters after this are an exploration of key trading concepts. In Chapter 3, I cover the nature of the markets, digging into the most popular traded markets and instruments. (The term 'instrument' is used throughout the book to represent any of the many assets that can be bought or sold on tradeable markets; i.e., anything that can be traded.) I also lay bare the underlying nature of market behavior. In Chapter 4, I share what you need to know about the major analytical techniques, fundamental and technical, as well as seasonality and wave theories. Chapter 5 provides an in-depth look at key trading techniques and styles.

Chapters 6 to 8 focus on developing a business plan and a trading plan, and sharing examples of successful trading plans. I discuss the components of a trader's 'edge'—how to find yours and how to maintain it, how to find a trading strategy aligned to your current profile, and how to document a plan that will form a solid foundation for your trading business.

In Chapter 9, I cover trading psychology, where I document some of the most common emotional mistakes that traders—both novice and experienced—make on a regular basis. These are mistakes that prevent long-term success and are responsible for destroying trading careers.

Chapter 10 brings together the key lessons, summarizing the major success factors I have learned over the years.

After finishing this book, you should have a good overview of the business of trading, be able to have an honest discussion with yourself about whether trading is right for you—and, if it is, be able to map out *and follow* a plan to long-term success. You will also be able to determine the style of trading that best fits your personality and be prepared for roadblocks you will encounter along the way. And you will have learned all the most valuable trading lessons I have acquired over a lifetime in the markets. Your journey will be well on the way, and your end destination all the closer.

Let's turn the page and ask an important question.

CHAPTER 1
IS TRADING REALLY FOR YOU?

MEET A LOT of people who say they are interested in trading. Once we start talking, though, I realize that all they are really interested in is making a lot of money in a short period of time. This is not trading.

The fact is, the vast majority of people driven by such a desire would be better off going to Vegas. The probability of making a few bucks is about the same, and at least they could take in a good show.

Trading is an extremely rewarding endeavor, if pursued with discipline. It is the ultimate marketplace of ideas; the right ones are profitable. And there is no limit to the amount you can make. But the only way big fortunes are made quickly in trading is the same way they are made at the roulette wheel: against the odds.

Unfortunately, most would-be traders are sold on the hype. They have unrealistic expectations. There are always going to be individuals who *do* suddenly strike it rich in the markets. But study their methods. Some may be naturals; most turn out to have assumed huge risk with leveraged instruments and lucked out. They didn't so much play with matches as juggle with dynamite. They survived—but it's not a party trick, much less a strategy for a career.

And for every such wild success story, there are thousands who lost it all. You usually won't read about them.

> **Many are drawn to trading for the supposed freedom. It is ironic that in order to succeed you must establish strict rules and boundaries.**

Trading appeals to our greed. There's no escaping it. The barriers to entry are all but nonexistent; almost anyone can open an account online within minutes, transfer some dollars from their bank account, and with a few keystrokes be in business. We are bombarded by rags-to-riches stories. We want to believe that they can be true for us too. Like sheep to slaughter, each year new traders enter the market—and lose their hard-earned capital, seeking easy money.

For most, the road to ruin is predictable. Something sparked their interest in trading—a story of easy money with little or no work, a hot tip from a friend or relative, an e-mail promising instant wealth, a news report of some spectacular run that a stock has just had. They urgently set up an account. They don't want to miss out. How much capital to deposit? It's obviously a 'sure thing'—so the more the better. Right?

The first trade is the easy one. Brokers always have a flavor of the day. Online, the next hot stock is just a click away. The outcome of that first trade will determine what happens next. Some pick a winner right off the bat. Sometimes a string of them! This beginner's luck reinforces all the messages that got them into trading. At this rate, they think they will make a fortune in no time.

They confuse luck with brains. So, it's not surprising that brains are missing from their next actions. Without any proper money-management rules, they pyramid their gains—until finally their luck runs out, and the house of cards comes tumbling down.

Others have a loss right out of the gate. That might be everything they could spare; in which case the game is over. Or they might attempt revenge on misfortune by trading again. Only to lose again. And worse.

Everyone who starts out trading this naively gets to the same place by different routes: inevitable loss of capital.

I have witnessed this scenario many times. It never ceases to amaze me how otherwise smart, rational individuals can get swept up by greed, ignoring all logic. They know loss is possible in a dictionary sense. But they never seem to consider it as a possibility in the trading sense. They will not listen to reason; they have it all under control. At some point, they finally realize that maybe there is more to this trading thing then they thought—but it is usually too late. They have lost too much money.

At this point, many give up on trading completely. The pain of losing large sums of money is too much. They never want to experience it again. This is too bad: many of them could have become successful traders if they had entered the business differently. For others, trading was never something they should have attempted in the first place. If they had spent some time beforehand understanding the business, they might have been able to avoid the inevitable losses.

How can a prospective trader work out into which group they fall? It starts with the simple question of this chapter:

Is trading really for you?

The reality is that trading is not for everyone, and an honest answer to this question may prevent a lot of pain in the long run. If trading *is* for you, this is far from a wasted exercise: by first looking objectively at what is involved, you will approach the business with your eyes wide open and be able to avoid a lot of the mistakes other traders make. Even if you're an experienced trader, it's helpful to really understand our motivations—and what actually makes for success.

To properly answer this question, what is needed is a cold hard look at yourself—and an honest and objective understanding of what truly is involved in the business of trading.

Let's break it down.

WHY DO YOU WANT TO TRADE?

Making money is what motivates most people to trade. After all, that is the ultimate goal of the business: using your capital to make money. However, if your main motivation is to make a *quick* killing, trading may not be for you. If time is of the essence, trading is going to prove an expensive lesson.

A lot of books on trading will tell you that trading is not gambling. I beg to differ. The definition of gambling is 'to bet on an uncertain outcome.' That sounds like trading to me. Sure, we will try and find an edge and minimize the possibility of loss—but, no matter what we do, the outcome will always be uncertain. And since we are being honest, let's not forget that there are dangers involved. Like other forms of gambling, trading can be addictive. I have seen many traders who 'need' to trade—but not in a good way. They need to trade, like other gamblers 'need' to bet. If you fear you may have a gambling problem or an addictive personality, trading may not be for you.

Most successful traders are passionate about the business, dedicating years to studying, gaining experience and knowledge over time. The activity in itself is an enormous part of the reward.

What is it about the idea of trading itself that appeals to you? Unless you are truly passionate about the business and willing to dedicate years to the endeavor, trading may not be for you.

For example, some of the most successful traders I know are driven to succeed in order to help fund charitable causes they support. It is interesting how this 'why' has such a powerful impact on their ability to stay focused and committed to their business, while others more easily fall prey to their emotions and lack staying power.

What is your 'why?'

WHAT ARE YOUR EXPECTATIONS?

For some reason, most new traders approach the business with expectations that are totally unrealistic. They think that learning to trade is automatic—as if it happens as soon as you open an account.

Greed seems to remove all rational thought. Like any new skill, trading requires dedication of time and practice. It will only be mastered over many years.

Not only do new traders not appreciate the time required to learn the business, but they also feel that earning positive returns on their capital should be a piece of cake. I have seen individuals decide to become day traders, thinking that they can easily earn $100,000 per year with only a $50,000 capital base. The logic goes something like this:

> With approximately 250 trading days a year, I only need to make $400 per day. With $50,000, that is less than a 1% move in a day. If I trade a $50 stock, it only needs to move to $50.50. This should be easy.

If this makes sense to you, maybe your expectations are unrealistic as well. It equates to a 200% return in a year.

I know a lot of successful traders who would consider an annual return of 20% to be exceptional. To earn $100,000 per year from that would require a capital base of $500,000. This helps to explain why new traders, in order to make the unrealistic returns they are expecting, gravitate towards highly leveraged instruments like futures and options, and assume huge risks. They are then easily wiped out. Figure 1.1 shows the equity curves of a successful trader and an average trader.

Figure 1.1: Equity curves

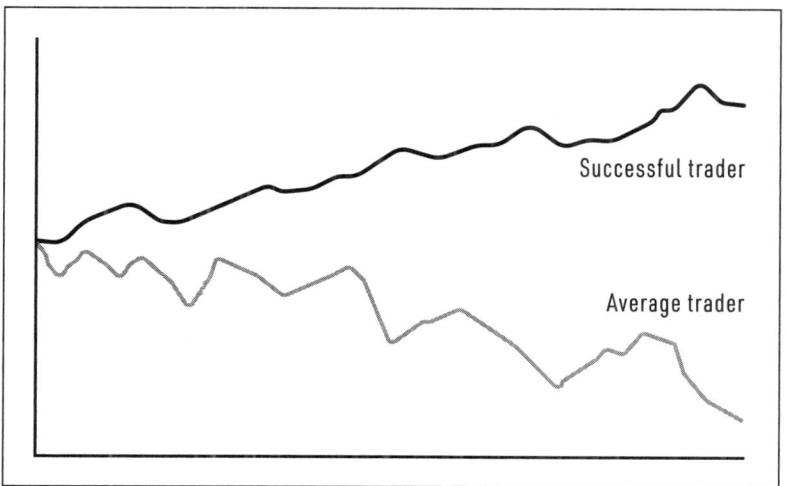

Source: Author.

If you're not prepared to devote serious time and practice to the art of trading, and would not be happy with objectively reasonable returns, trading may not be for you.

WHAT DOES IT TAKE TO BECOME A SUCCESSFUL TRADER?

Before anyone can expect to become successful at any profession, they need to dedicate time to learning the fundamentals and practicing the skill set. Most professions take years to master; trading is no exception.

But trading also has an emotional component. The same is *not* true for most other professions. This is one of the most critical aspects of trading, and one that is usually missed by most people. Emotional resilience is critical—and critically overlooked.

Then there's passion. One of the first things people advise when choosing a profession is to 'do what you love.' Most successful traders I know are extremely passionate about what they do. They dedicate many hours a day to their trading business; before, during and after trading hours.

> **Many new traders leave the game once they realize the amount of work and time commitment involved, and after their expectations of easy money are shattered.**

Most who approach the business successfully have higher than average intelligence, are mathematically inclined and are computer literate. They are independent thinkers and are able to make decisions on their own. They are comfortable working in isolation but also have a passion for understanding group psychology. But, above all, they love the markets, and they love trading.

WHY SHOULD YOU LEARN TO TRADE?

While it may appear that I am trying to convince people to stay away from trading, this is not the case. I just want people who come to trading looking for a get-rich-quick scheme to understand what trading actually is, and what successful trading actually takes. No one who pretends that trading will quickly make you rich is doing you a favor or bringing your success any closer.

I actually believe that *everyone* should learn the basics of trading and investing. That much should be a fundamental component of secondary education. Our education system focuses on so many areas that ultimately provide little help for the average person during their lifetime. We live in a capitalistic system—but do not have mandatory education on business, economics and investing. This is shocking. (I feel the same way about parenting, nutrition and relationships.)

Most individuals entering adulthood are confronted with major financial decisions that they are grossly unprepared to make. They need to rely on the advice of others, whose interests are often not aligned with theirs. Not knowing any better, they follow blindly and often pay a devastating price for their ignorance.

Then, when people get older and accumulate savings, they hand over their money to a 'professional' to manage, thinking that they will look after them. Although there are some very competent money managers out there, there is often a noticeable disconnect between what they promise and what they deliver. In every bear market that I have lived through, I have seen many lose great chunks of their investment portfolios. Often with severe consequences, such as having to postpone retirement, divorce, deteriorating health—and, in extreme cases, death. They had their funds invested, with no clue as to the risks that they were taking.

All monies committed to the markets have to be *watched*—and the only one who really cares, and who ultimately has to live with the consequences, is *you*. It is your money, your decisions—and, therefore, your consequences.

You may not have the time or interest to learn to trade, but I would recommend that everyone at least commits to learning some of the basics of lower-risk, longer-term investing.

THE NEXT STEP

My objective with this chapter was to have every trader, old and new, ask themselves some difficult questions, so that they can approach the business of trading with eyes wide open. Most approach it with tunnel vision.

Without a realistic evaluation of what trading entails, people's pocketbooks will take a hard hit. If, after this evaluation, you decide trading is not for you, then by avoiding it you will be saving yourself from significant losses and emotional turmoil. For those who decide trading is for them, you now have a better idea of what you need for long-term success.

Are you willing to dedicate the time, energy and capital to make a serious go of this business? If so, then developing a proper education plan is the next step. We'll piece that together now.

CHAPTER 2
A TRADER'S EDUCATION

DESPITE BEING A lifelong trader, I can honestly say that not a day goes by in which I do not learn something new about myself or about the market. The market is the great leveler, ever changing, requiring everyone who engages with it to be constantly on their toes. Every time you trade, the market forces you to look in the mirror, revealing every flaw and blemish in your practice. You cannot hide from this reality—you must be willing to face it and to change if you are ever to meet the requirements the market demands.

Every trade you make—whether it is a winning or losing one—will expose flaws in your intellectual and emotional approach to the market. How you respond to these revelations is crucial.

Traders who refuse to face this painful reality lose fast and hard, sooner or later. They fail to learn the lessons the market reveals to them, and eventually most abandon the market, never to return. Those who accept that they are flawed will still lose sometimes, but they lick their wounds and evolve over time. If you want to join the ranks of these experienced survivors, you need to arm yourself with the proper educational tools.

I will show you the tools you need and how to use them. But I also want you to ask yourself this important question: "How much time do I want to spend suffering?"

FAILING TO PLAN IS PLANNING TO FAIL

The typical evolution of a trader is slow and painful to watch. New traders tend to read a couple of books on the subject and think they are experts. They make a few trades and soon realize that they have a lot more to learn—but most look to further their education in the wrong places. They seek advice on specific trades, but they fail to gain a broader understanding of trading. They switch from stocks to options, penny stocks to futures, always looking for the right instrument to trade, instead of trying to find the right trading approach for them. They listen to the so-called 'experts'—talking heads, gurus, newsletters and blogs—and yet they continue to be frustrated with their results. Eventually they realize that most of the time, the experts' calls are wrong.

After this has gone on for a while, often accompanied by moderate to serious losses, the evolving trader takes a more serious look at trading books and courses, and usually tries to adopt someone else's methodology, even though it usually does not feel right for them. The methodology may involve accepting price fluctuations that feel too substantial or trading over a timeframe that is too short, requiring too much hands-on intervention, for example. Around this time the trader starts to understand that success will not be found at the feet of any one particular authority—instead, they must synthesize a great many lessons in order to develop a set of rules that *they* feel comfortable with.

This is an important evolutionary leap, but it is far from the end goal. Around this time the trader returns to their books, seeking to better understand the key principles they will work into their own personal trading plan. Usually at this point, the systems they develop are extremely complex. They back test—assessing their strategy against historical data—and go live, only to find themselves confused by conflicting signals.

Again, the trader meets will failure, but if they push through and continue to evolve, they find themselves reconsidering some earlier assumptions. Returning to the drawing board, this time they cut away the confusing complexity and develop a simple system that works for them.

However, even with a simple approach, they find that they are breaking the rules every time. They just do not seem to be making progress. Fear of failure (and the paradoxical fear of success), risk aversion, and lack of discipline are just some of the psychological issues that may be holding them back and preventing them from following their own simple set of rules.

Finally, the trader commits to a plan of self-improvement, tackling the hardest part of trading: themselves. Only once they understand themselves—their triggers and motives, strengths and weaknesses, biases, fears, warts and all—do they finally start to experience consistent success in trading.

> **Your odds of success increase dramatically when you replace greed and impatience with study and discipline.**

I have seen traders walk this path for decades without ever reaching this final stage. If they were honest with themselves from the beginning and had asked "Is trading for me?" most would have answered no and would never have begun trading in the first place. Others lacked proper training and education plans, and continued to struggle on their own, trying to reinvent the wheel. Of those who *do* implement a plan, a great many have the potential to achieve success but miss critical components needed to ensure consistent profitability and long-term success. Often overlooked is the development of plans that a) ensure they are aligned with the strategy they want to trade and b) develop the proper mindset to build the psychological resilience necessary to implement their strategy effectively.

I'll assume you don't want to suffer as much as these aspiring traders do, so let's examine how to avoid these pitfalls.

KNOWLEDGE → EXPERIENCE → SKILL

Ultimately, everyone comes to their first trade with a unique combination of life experience and knowledge. Whatever yours may be, I urge you to step back and honestly evaluate what you know—versus what you think you know—before you commit to that first trade.

CHAPTER 2

From my experience, your level of academic education or achievement is not a key determinant of your chance of success as a trader. Passion, determination, discipline and emotional intelligence seem to be more important than a person's IQ. A lot of very intelligent individuals approach the business thinking that it will be a piece of cake. They are well-educated professionals with extensive business knowledge, but they often lack the emotional fortitude to succeed or are too arrogant to acknowledge their weaknesses.

Others with less experience and education tend to approach trading with the proper level of modesty and humility, accepting whatever lessons the market gives them. Wherever you are on the spectrum between these two points, it is important to approach trading with the seriousness that it deserves. Fortunately, there is a tried and tested way to approach this business and that is with a proper education plan. This plan should include a combination of book learning (accumulating knowledge), analysis (gaining experience), and actual time spent trading (honing the skill).

1. First a new trader must study, to ensure they understand the key components and fundamentals of trading. These are the basic rules of the game that all market participants need before they place their first trade.

2. The next step is conducting analyses of the markets, to which the trader can apply the concepts they have studied, in order to get a better feel for how they function. Through this process they develop a level of experience of—and familiarity with—market fluctuations, patterns, and temperaments that they can later utilize in their live trading.

3. Thirdly, a new trader must engage in *actual trading*, to test and refine the theoretical skills they have developed. Their

introduction to trading must be carefully managed, starting with small-size, low-risk, low-volatility trades, in order to get their feet wet and gain a feel for the emotional component of trading. The trader can then build up to the size and style of trading that their education has helped them identify as best fitting their personality.

Let's unpack each of these concepts in more detail.

BOOK LEARNING (KNOWLEDGE)

The good news is that there is currently an unending supply of information and resources available to anyone interested in learning the fundamentals of the trading business. There are a number of classic works that act as a great starting point, and of course the internet has enough material to keep someone busy for a lifetime.

Most people think they just need to learn a few trading rules and they are in business. It is usually only over time that they begin to realize the complexity involved in trading. The best approach is to identify the key areas of study and develop a learning plan around the gaps in your existing knowledge.

Some of the main areas of study I recommend your learning include:

- Brokerage accounts
- Computer systems and programs
- Types of markets to trade
- Types of instruments to trade
- Trading styles and systems
- Money management
- Trader psychology
- Fundamental analysis
- Technical analysis

In the next few chapters I provide a primer on these areas, offering advice on what to focus on, with an emphasis on critical decisions to be made. How quickly you can integrate the key learning points depends on how you approach the task and how much time and money you are willing to invest in your education.

You can either develop a self-learning plan using free resources on the internet and library or invest in a more formal method of study. The key in either case is to make sure you are studying the best material and using legitimate sources. I recommend you stay away from any 'get-rich-quick' promotions you come across and focus on more credible sources.

I recommend some classic trading texts throughout this book and provide a convenient list of them in the Recommended Reading section at the back. I suggest you begin by reading a handful of these to provide you with a solid foundation. This will help you to make better choices going forward. I believe that self-learning is a great option from my experience, but it can only take you to a certain level and it proceeds at a much slower pace than taking formal courses.

There are many successful traders out there who are willing to share their experience and knowledge. Nothing beats a trading coach or mentor to help accelerate your learning curve and ensure you have a firm grasp on the material you are studying. However, many new traders decide not to involve a formal coach or mentor because of the expense involved. Most usually end up paying many times the value of this 'tuition fee' in the form of losses, once they begin to trade. They are forced to learn from mistakes that they otherwise may have avoided, had they received the proper guidance.

There are also many online and in-person trading groups available now, and these are a great resource for meeting fellow traders, getting referrals and recommendations for training material, and sharing lessons amongst the group. I have stated that trading is a lonely business, a solitary game where you live or die by the decisions *you* make. However, it is great to have a group of like-minded traders to associate with and to share experiences and knowledge.

> **Many are attracted to trading to 'be their own boss' but find that not having a boss to mentor and guide them is actually a gap. Finding other traders to share goals and experiences can help fill this gap and help accelerate your learning.**

If you are serious about this business, I recommend that you take this phase of your training seriously and invest the time and money needed to get the best education you can. It will save you large amounts of money in the long run.

ANALYSIS (EXPERIENCE)

Imagine that you have now read a number of books, taken some courses and perhaps met other traders or coaches—we'll assume that by this point you have a reasonable understanding of the fundamentals of trading. This is when you need to take what you

CHAPTER 2

have learned and implement it. First you need to put in some screen time, and lots of it. By screen time, I mean looking at charts.

It is important to commit a good deal of time to studying historical and current charts, using them to review all the material that you have learned to date. Study various chart types, different time frames, price-volume relationships, trend lines, support and resistance, indicators, and market cycles, until these concepts are ingrained into your brain. (Don't panic if these terms are completely alien to you now, we'll cover them all in Chapter 4.)

You'll soon become intimately acquainted with charts much like the one in Figure 2.1.

Figure 2.1: Daily chart example

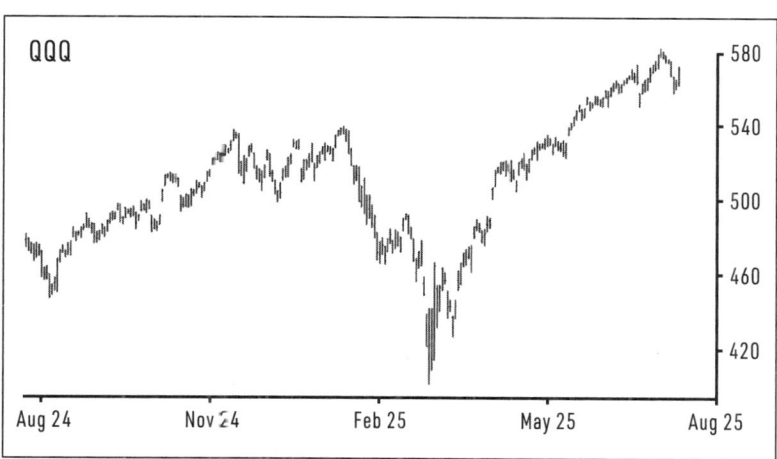

Source: TrendSpider.

This is a daily chart of the Invesco QQQ Trust ETF (QQQ)—a popular exchange-traded fund (hence 'ETF').

Note that there are 12 months of trading data contained in this chart, with each bar representing one day of trading activity. This differentiates it from intraday charts, the other type you'll become very familiar with. Intraday charts break each daily price movement into smaller time frames (like 30 minutes per bar), so allow you to track much shorter-term fluctuations.

Eventually, you will be determining what markets, instruments and time frames to trade in, but for now, you should study as many different markets and instruments as you can. Study commodities (metals, financial and grains), study stocks (international, domestic, blue chips and penny stocks) and study bonds (government and commercial). You can review and get a feeling for any market that exists. Also study multiple time frames (yearly, monthly, weekly, 60 minutes, 30 minutes and five minutes).

Initially you will just be reinforcing the materials you have studied until you truly understand them. Go over each concept, studying the charts, until it becomes second nature to you. You want to get to a point where you can glance at a chart and quickly have a feel for what is going on. Practice, practice, practice. Just like most traders, you will eventually see charts in your sleep. When you look at a chart, you will immediately know if it is trending or in a trading range, if there are any critical price-volume changes, if any major patterns are forming, what the significant support and resistance areas are and whether it is overbought or oversold.

Finally, you will be able to answer the most important question of all: should you go long on this trade (buying with the expectation of selling after the price rises, go short (selling with the expectation of buying after the price falls), or stand aside (waiting for a clear signal)?

CHAPTER 2

What you will also learn—and what you must commit to memory—is that nothing works 100% of the time.

So many books will teach you a methodology and give numerous examples of trades that worked, while ignoring the many that failed. Novices reading these books begin to imagine how easy it will be to rake in the big bucks. They find a bullish pattern and go long or recognize an apparent opportunity they've recently learned about—let's say a moving average crossover buy signal—only to see that these setups don't always play out like they do in the books. In reality, sometimes they work and other times they fail miserably. Analyzing the market through the lens of your newly acquired knowledge will open your eyes to these possibilities and prepare you for the next phase of your education: gaining real trading experience and understanding the difficult psychological challenges associated with trading.

Studying financial news and trends will not only help to reinforce the concepts you have learned, but you will also start to get a better feel for what style of trading appeals to you the most. As you learn about trading, you will often hear that you need to find a trading style that fits *you* personally. It is critically important to find a trading approach that is aligned to your personality, lifestyle, knowledge, and experience. One that matches your risk tolerance, as well as your overall comfort level. You should factor in your time commitment, financial goals, available capital, personality type, and emotional resilience.

Unfortunately, most novice traders simply pick the style that they think will make them the most money in the shortest period of time; or they jump on the first trading methodology that they learn about, eager to get trading as soon as possible.

Part of your formal education should include reading about other traders and their methodologies. If you are truly passionate about trading, this will be an ongoing exercise. There are a number of great books that profile traders and their styles, such as the classic *Market Wizards* series, by Jack D. Schwager. You can also follow successful traders on social media.

Reading and following successful traders is a great motivator. You will soon realize that there are as many different trading styles and methodologies as there are traders. Each person brings to the business their own unique style and flair. Like artists, traders spend time learning the fundamentals of the craft before developing a style unique unto themselves. There truly is no one right way to trade.

The more you study other traders and are exposed to different methodologies, the more you will gravitate towards a certain style that you feel comfortable with. Focus on this preferred style—follow those traders who also trade this way and perfect it. You may find that your particular focus works better in certain market environments than it does in others. For example, the perennial bear (who believes stock prices will decline and seeks to take advantage of that) will struggle during a bull market (in which prices rise) and must stand aside.

As traders gain experience, they may find themselves adding more and more styles to their repertoire, each of which can be deployed during the appropriate market environments. Others will stick to their tried-and-true methods for life. Again, there is no right way to trade, there are only ways that work for you and ways that don't. As a novice, however, it is critical to find one style that you are drawn to, study it, document it, and ready yourself for the next phase, where you begin to trade.

CHAPTER 2

TRADING EXPERIENCE (SKILL)

Let's suppose that you have now learned the basics, put in lots of screen time and picked a trading methodology that you are aligned with. You have also documented your business and trading plan, and have 'paper traded'—practiced without committing your own money—for some time. This has honed your skill for finding trading opportunities, and you have diligently documented these trades and kept your trading journal up to date.

You should have confidence in your abilities, at least on paper. If you also have your office set up, a brokerage account open, and your internet connection in place, you are finally ready for the real trading experience. At this point the book learning ends, and real trading begins.

I will be the first to say that you will only truly learn the art of trading by *actually trading*. Paper trading is great for helping to hone your analytic skills, but it does little to develop the emotional aspects of the business. Like any other new skill, especially where there is risk involved, you really need to walk before you run, and with trading, I would even suggest beginning at a crawl.

A closer analogy is the process of learning to drive. A person does not just decide they want to drive and then immediately get behind the wheel and drive out onto the highway, at least not without causing an accident. They first practice going up and down the driveway, then graduate to an empty parking lot, then try out a quiet side street and eventually, after building up their skills and experience, they finally enter the highway with the big boys and girls. I would suggest a similar approach to trading.

By now you are part-way through this learning process. You are ready to get behind the wheel, put it in drive and experience the physical and—more importantly—emotional side of the business. With all of the groundwork you have completed, you are now in a much better position than the average new trader.

Most new traders have bypassed these foundational steps, opened an account and placed a trade, only to find that as soon as they start, they crash and burn. You are farther ahead of the game and much more prepared to engage in a long-term trading experience, because you took your time to build up the essential trading skills, step by step. Taking this approach required discipline and patience, two of the most important traits of a successful trader. Trust me when I say that this hard work will pay off in the long run! It will help you to avoid the huge emotional swings most traders encounter and to establish a routine that will help to keep you on track.

Another big mistake that novice traders make is basing their decisions on their emotions (primarily greed and fear) instead of logic. You, on the other hand, have studied a number of markets and instruments, have found a trading methodology you like and a time frame you want to trade in. This sets you up for a greater chance of success.

It is more important at this point to develop basic trading skills, reinforcing discipline and confronting your emotional reactions—all while taking on the lowest possible risk—than to make money. For this reason, I would recommend trading a longer time frame (at least daily), with a low-volatility instrument and a very small position size (i.e., invest only a little money in something that is unlikely to bounce between jarring highs and lows).

The goal here is not to *make* a lot of money, the goal is to not *lose* a lot of money. This will enable you to learn and begin to master the emotional rollercoaster of trading. I cover the most common emotional issues that traders face in Chapter 9, but at this point just accept that you will experience emotions that, until they are under better control, can cause traders to make the worst possible decisions. They make them break their own rules and often result in losses. You will find it much easier to master your reactions to these emotions if you have kept risk to a minimum.

You will have noticed that when you were paper trading, not all trades were winners. You followed your rules, put in your stops, and sometimes—but not always—everything worked out as planned. When losses were incurred, you moved on. They had little impact on your ability to trade. Accepting these failures is not so easy when actual dollars are on the line. Facing the fact that some trades will be losers, and doing what is required when they turn against you, requires true confidence in your plan. This confidence can only be gained over time—and with actual dollars at risk.

There is an emotional consideration that must be understood when choosing the time frame over which to trade. There is an inverse relationship between the length of the time frame and the level of emotional investment, so trading over shorter time frames leads to more complex emotional entanglement with our trades.

Trading a shorter time frame to capture profits really is a double-edged sword—it can lead to huge gains for those who do it well, but can take huge chunks out of your account if you let your focus wander.

Also, the shorter the time frame, the more screen time involved and the larger chance for errors. Each time you are exposed to the screen and facing the consequences of your decisions, the more likely you are to second guess your rules and break them. You may be able to avoid this trap by trading off a daily or weekly chart, reviewing and adjusting your trades as little as once per day.

Of course, your rules also need to ensure you don't go too far the other way—that you don't just buy and wait for profits to accumulate. It is amazing how quickly short-term traders become long-term investors with a portfolio of losing open positions. I have seen them waiting to sell a sinking stock once it gets back to their entry price, hoping to break even at best. It is more likely that losses will continue to grow until they cannot take it any longer and sell—usually at the low. This stems from not having a pre-defined stop level (the point at which the trader has decided they will 'exit' a trade by selling). This is one of the biggest mistakes traders make. Short-term traders become accidental investors when the stock goes against them.

When you're fishing, you keep your line in the water waiting for the big fish to hit, but you need to know how to reel it in. Being able to take a small loss at a predefined exit point is critical.

Regardless of where you get your trade ideas, you won't make any money until *you* buy and sell. *You* pull the trigger when *you* enter and when *you* exit. It is *you* that will ultimately determine your own success or failure.

If you've read any other trading books, you may have noticed that they always labor the point "Do not trade with money you cannot afford to lose." What this really means is that you should be prepared to kiss the money you commit to your first live trades goodbye. With the proper approach this does not have to be the case. You need to understand and manage the risks you are exposing yourself to. Initially focus on protecting your capital before you start to focus on making profits.

A trader who cannot sleep at night, has anxiety, loss of concentration, mercurial mood swings or is depressed (and can ascribe these symptoms to no other cause) has probably exceeded their risk tolerance. If this sounds like you, then you have probably also either broken your money management rules or have found yourself on the wrong side of a gap that has well exceeded your stop level. If none of these are true, then you just may be uncomfortable with the size of your trading account. Whatever the case may be, you need to either reduce the dollar amount you have allocated for trading or trade less volatile instruments, until you get your comfort level and confidence back.

While any book of this type can tell you how to be a successful trader, many people do not have the discipline to succeed. The basics are simple: no matter what instrument you decide to trade, once you purchase it, it can either go up, down or sideways. That's it. If it goes down and you sell, you have lost money. If it goes up and you sell, you have made money. If it goes sideways and you sell, you have only incurred the transaction costs, neither making nor losing money on the trade. What could be simpler?

I love that trading is so simple, yet hate that it is so hard. Now that you understand the first steps you'll take on your trader's journey and have a solid education plan in place, let's turn our attention to the companion who will be with you every step of the way—the markets.

CHAPTER 3
THE NATURE OF THE MARKETS

ONE OF THE first steps along the trader's journey is to gain a firm grasp of the basics of the markets. Here we review their key components at a high level. A trader's education never ends, so this exercise is important whether it serves as an introduction to new concepts (if you're just starting out as a trader) or an opportunity to step back and review your understanding (if you're already trading).

WHAT IS THE MARKET?

People tend to think that 'trading' begins and ends with stocks and the stock market. This is what they are most exposed to in the media, with the status of the Dow Jones, Nasdaq, and S&P 500 quoted regularly throughout the day and specific company results quoted daily. When you enter the world of trading, however, you soon learn that there are many markets and hundreds, if not thousands, of instruments to trade.

But let's focus on the familiar stock market, also known as the equity market. To understand the nature of the equity market, we must first begin with the basics. What *is* the market?

In a capitalistic system, companies are created to produce products and provide services. Creating a company requires funds, and there are a number of ways to raise money. Companies can borrow money or raise equity by selling part-ownership in the business. Depending on the size and goals of the business, they may decide to do this privately or publicly. If they decide to do this publicly, the proportion of the company to be sold (its 'stock') is divided up into units called 'shares', which are listed on an exchange from which they can be bought and sold. (While technically a 'share' refers to a single instance of a company's 'stock,' the terms are often used interchangeably.)

Each exchange has different qualifiers and rules that companies must meet in order to get listed initially and remain listed. Anything tradable on an exchange is assigned a 'ticker', which is a three-or-four-letter code unique to that instrument (for example, Apple's ticker is AAPL). We'll see a few examples of tickers elsewhere in the book.

Essentially the equity market is made up of all the shares of the publicly listed companies on the various exchanges. In the US, for example, we have two major exchanges: the New York Stock Exchange and the Nasdaq. Smaller public companies who would not qualify for listing on either of these exchanges can trade 'over the counter' (OTC), which is a direct trade conducted without the oversight of an exchange.

CHAPTER 3

When the market and I disagree, the market always wins.

When most people talk about 'the markets,' they are not usually referring to *all* markets collectively or even to the entire 'universe' of stocks, but to a stock index they are familiar with, such as the Dow Jones, Nasdaq Composite, or S&P 500. The performance of these indices is what is quoted most often in market news. Each index measures the value of a group or segment of stocks. The Dow Jones, Nasdaq Composite, and S&P 500 are three broad-based indices that reflect the performance of the overall markets. Other indices track the performance of discrete industry sectors or global regions. Indices reflect the overall market performance of the sector they track and are often used as a benchmark against which to measure the relative performance of individual instruments.

Figure 3.1 shows the Invesco QQQ Trust ETF, going back over the last five years. You can clearly see the major 'bull' and 'bear' cycles, as markets rise and fall respectively. This fund tracks the performance of the Nasdaq-100 index, so represents some of the largest and most innovative technology companies in the US. Indices therefore represent the major economic cycles of the country or countries they track. If you view other, more specific sector indices, you can gauge where they are in their respective cycles.

Figure 3.1: Economic cycles

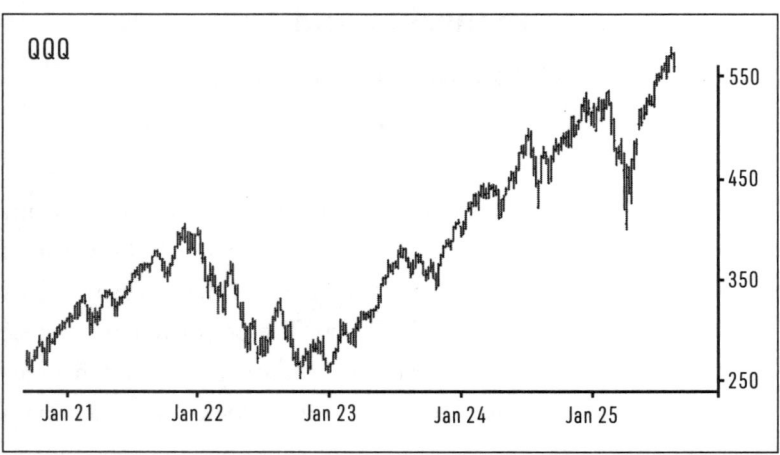

Source: TrendSpider.

The equity market (where stocks are traded) is just the tip of the iceberg. There are also the forex market (where foreign exchange is traded), bond market (where loans in the form of bonds are traded), futures market (contracts for future trades), and commodities market (for commodities from gold to cattle).

WHAT CAN YOU TRADE IN THE MARKET?

There are countless different instruments to trade across the various markets, ranging from individual shares, options, currencies, commodities, and futures contracts to collected baskets of individual instruments held in mutual funds and ETFs. Each instrument has its own characteristics of volatility, liquidity, and market capitalization (amongst many more), so there are many variables to consider.

CHAPTER 3

Picking the right instrument to trade is an important step in a trader's journey. Like choosing your trading style, the instrument you choose to trade must fit your personality. By studying the various options available and their major characteristics you may find yourself drawn to one area or group that you feel more comfortable with.

One thing to keep in mind when deciding what to trade is that some instruments are inherently riskier than others and it is easy to be swayed by this. Most beginners are looking for the quick road to riches and are drawn to the most-leveraged instruments from the start. Of course, that is another reason most beginners' accounts are wiped out in no time. Picking your trading instrument should initially be based on other factors. As you develop as a trader you will have an opportunity to graduate to more volatile and highly leveraged instruments.

Though there are literally thousands of instruments to choose from, as you spend time studying charts you will soon see that there are major groups of charts that look practically identical. In a way, markets behave like the ocean, with rising and falling tides creating an overall macro-picture of that market. Waves represent significant trends, and ripples represent minor changes. Essentially major groups of instruments will trade in sync with each other (creating tides), while the size of the waves and ripples will differ because of their own unique characteristics.

Using gold stocks as an example of this macro analogy, imagine gold stocks as a group. They will rise and fall in sync with the overall trends in the underlying value of gold. While this major trend will have a huge impact on gold stocks, the value of each stock will still differ from comparable stocks because of characteristics unique to each company that forms part of the market.

So, you can compare a large-cap gold company (one with a large market capitalization, or overall market value), with a large reserve of gold properties, that trades almost in sync with gold itself or a small-cap, highly leveraged gold mine, which will be much more volatile. The major difference in how these two companies will trade is a statistical term called 'beta,' which measures the relative sensitivity of an instrument to a market movement. Essentially, if the value of gold goes up 1%, some companies that move in sync with gold will see their value grow faster than others. The bottom line is that there are major groups of instruments that trade in sync with each other, and some make bigger swings while others make lesser moves.

One other factor to consider when deciding which markets to trade in is the time of day during which the relevant exchanges are open. There are many exchanges around the world and each has its own trading hours. Although the North American exchanges are the largest markets by market capitalization (the total value of the companies traded there) there are also major exchanges in Europe, Asia, India, and the Middle East. Your decision may be impacted by where you live and what time you have available to trade.

Let's take a whistle-stop tour through the main categories of markets and trading instruments, to give you a flavor of their major characteristics.

STOCKS

Let's face it, most traders are originally drawn to 'stocks and shares'. This is the one investment area that most people are exposed to through the media. We are constantly bombarded with stock market statistics and corporate news announcements. We are also keenly aware as consumers what is going on with the companies we shop at. Many people also have invested in stocks through their mutual funds, pension plans and retirement savings plans.

Stocks can be categorized in a number of different ways, each grouping them by a distinct characteristic. One common way that stocks are grouped is by their market capitalization size. Small-cap stocks (in companies with a total value under about $2 billion), mid-cap stocks (about $2–10bn), and large-cap stocks (anything over $10bn).

In addition to market capitalization, traders often look at the sectors that companies belong to. Sectors group companies that share common products or services together. The S&P breaks the market into 11 sectors: utilities, consumer staples, transportation, technology, health care, financial, energy, consumer cyclicals, basic materials, capital goods, and communications.

BONDS

When governments and corporations need funds, they often issue bonds. These are essentially loans that need to be paid back over a specified period of time, ranging from short-term treasury notes to long-term corporate bonds. Although there are no specific exchanges where bonds are traded (unlike stocks), they can be traded through banks and brokers. It is also possible to trade futures contracts for bonds and to include bonds within ETFs.

FOREIGN EXCHANGE (FOREX)

The foreign exchange market is where foreign currencies are traded. Most countries have a 'floating' exchange rate that determines the relative value of their currency at any point in time based on its supply and demand. In this market, one country's currency can be purchased or sold using the currency of another country.

The foreign exchange market is the largest asset class, in terms of trading volume, where trillions of dollars' worth of transactions can occur each day. Similar to the futures market, the players include those who actually need the currencies, like governments, banks, and commercial companies. There are also traders who are strictly there to speculate.

Trading the forex market is completely different to trading shares. This market is open 24 hours a day, there are no commissions, and the leverage is very high, with only a small deposit required to trade a large position. This can make it a risky proposition, best suited to experienced traders. For those experienced enough and interested in trading foreign currencies, there are futures contracts available in this market as well.

FUTURES AND COMMODITIES

Similar to the stock exchange, where shares of companies are transacted, there are commodity exchanges where 'futures' contracts are traded. These are places where producers and consumers of commodities (as well as speculators, of course) transact.

Unlike stocks, which can be held indefinitely, a number of commodities are produced and consumed, or used in production, over the course of a seasonal cycle. They are also produced in large quantities. The transactions are made through a contract for a fixed quantity of goods that gives the purchaser the obligation to purchase at the time of expiry.

Futures are similar to options, except that the buyer is obliged to fulfill the contracted transaction. Future contracts are standardized with fixed quantities, prices, expiry dates and margin requirements. They exist for commodities, as well as for a number of other financial instruments. Many are drawn to the futures market because of the leverage available, which allows a small amount of capital to control a large portfolio.

MUTUAL FUNDS

Mutual funds were originally created to give people the ability to invest in pools of professionally managed investments. Each fund is formed of a 'basket' of stocks, and when you buy into a mutual fund you are buying a share of that basket. The fund's manager will select the shares that are bought and added to the fund—for a fee. The sheer number of investments that make up a mutual fund means they offer diversification that otherwise may be hard to achieve for smaller investors.

Mutual funds tend to be created around one or more themes, such as growth, diversification, small-cap, large-cap, or international markets.

Mutual funds do not trade on stock exchanges, but are purchased through financial institutions, banks, insurance companies as well as directly. They are bought and sold at the net asset value (NAV), which is calculated daily.

ETFS

The latest creation of tradable instruments is the exchange-traded fund, better known as the ETF. Like a mutual fund, an ETF is formed of a basket of investments, but instead of being professionally managed they automatically track an index and hold the same investments that the index contains.

Investors in mutual funds are always struggling to find managers that, after management fees are taken off, can outperform the index their fund is benchmarked against and are often disappointed when they are unsuccessful. Often they would have been better off if they had just bought an index-tracking fund. ETFs were initially created to fill this void. They offer a lot of the same benefits of mutual funds and have addressed a lot of the limitations.

Unlike mutual funds, ETFs are traded directly on the stock exchange. Since they trade on the exchange, you always know their value. Since the only management involved is to mirror the index, the fees are minimal compared to mutual funds.

There are literally hundreds of ETFs to choose from. Like stocks, they fall into various sectors. Some of the most active ETFs track the S&P 500 and are known as the spider (ticker: SPY), Nasdaq knows them as the Qs (QQQ), and the Dow knows them as the diamonds (DIA).

OPTIONS

An 'option' gives its buyer the right to purchase a fixed number of shares at a fixed price (the 'strike price') at a date in the future. The buyer must speculate on the likely future price of the shares and determine whether the option price will be a good one relative to the actual price of those shares at the same point in the future.

There are a number of sophisticated strategies that combine the buying and selling of options, and they offer traders an endless number of ways to trade. It is an area that requires much study and experience to master.

Many traders buy options to increase their leverage and sell them to enhance their returns. Options are also an instrument that many new traders blow up their accounts with. You will often hear people saying that buying options is great because they have limited downside risk, with unlimited upside potential. This is true, but what they don't mention is that the limited downside risk is much more likely to be realized, since options are a wasting asset that lose part of their value every day, as they approach expiry.

CRYPTOCURRENCIES

I would be remiss if I did not include cryptocurrencies in my list of markets and instruments to trade. Though they had a shaky start, these latest additions to the markets are gaining popularity and are being taken seriously by many traders.

Crypto trading only began in 2009, with the creation of Bitcoin. For a long time after that, traders tended to avoid crypto because they did not understand it and the market for trading it lacked security and regulation.

From humble beginnings in 2009, when Bitcoin was the only instrument in this market, there are now thousands of cryptocurrencies available to trade. The market itself had grown to over $1 trillion by 2021. Suffice it to say I witnessed many horror stories and a few successes along the way. The evolution of these new and exciting assets, that can offer huge opportunities and huge returns, has been amazing to see, and over the last decade many traders have been drawn to them.

SPOILED FOR CHOICE

Once you determine what broad instruments you want to *follow*, you then need to decide which specific ones to *trade*. This again is a very personal decision that must fit your personality.

Some traders are continuously on the lookout for a new setup that fits their parameters, keeping track of the whole universe of instruments and striking when they see an opportunity. For example, for equities traders, their preparation might begin by screening through a large number of stocks, either visually or using a screening program. There are a number of great programs available that allow for both fundamental and technical screening (more on these topics in the next chapter) to help narrow down their list. Like fair-weather friends, as the markets change, the list of stocks that these traders would consider will also change. The important point is not what company or specific instrument gets identified, but that it meets very specific criteria at the time that they trade it.

Other traders identify a group of stocks from which they will trade exclusively. They still may have common characteristics, for example all may have large daily volumes, belong to the same industry, be large-cap stocks, etc. These traders become friends with their preferred stocks, getting to know all about them by following their every move. They still wait for their proper signal to trade, but do not venture from this group.

Finally, there are some traders that become true specialists and trade only one instrument. This is like having one best friend, where they rely solely on that one instrument to play with. This is often the case for day traders, but I have also seen position traders that make their living off only one instrument, such as oil or the S&P, for example.

CHOOSING YOUR INSTRUMENT

We have now covered the broad categories of tradable instruments. Once you decide on the category you want to trade from, the next step is to determine which specific instruments you want within that category.

Some categories, like futures and forex, are traditionally thought to be very risky and dangerous to trade because of their higher volatility and low margin requirements (the percentage of an instrument you must pay for up front). New traders are usually told to avoid these markets.

I would argue that within any market there are both safe and dangerous instruments. There are extremes in volatility within each category, and a novice can start out by choosing a safer instrument to cut their teeth and avoid the more volatile ones. Of course, most new traders ignore this advice and are drawn to the action, but they soon get wiped out. I have seen many new traders in the stock market go straight in for penny stocks, which can be more dangerous than futures contracts. This rarely ends well.

There are advantages and disadvantages to trading any market, and, like the markets, your trading instrument must fit your personality. New traders may want to focus on instruments with low volatility and high liquidity within their chosen market.

> # There is no best stock or instrument to trade. You must find the instrument that fits your specific goals and risk tolerance.

There are a number of ways to evaluate volatility. Some are very easy, and others are very sophisticated. Essentially, volatility is a measure of the price variation over a period of time. As a trader, the greater the volatility, the greater the opportunity to capture profits; but also, the greater the risk of loss if you are on the wrong side of the move.

A simple method to gauge the historic volatility of an instrument is to calculate the range between its 52-week high price point and its 52-week low. A higher-volatility stock will have a wider range than a lower-volatility one. Looking at a fairly long period of time like this will give you a good starting estimation of the instrument's volatility. Of course, volatility will fluctuate over time and can change significantly, so be sure to keep reviewing your findings.

Volatility and fluctuations over time are, unfortunately, important elements that many traders ignore. They are then often taken by surprise when things move faster than expected. Looking at multiple charts that have the same setups forming can be very deceptive when trying to anticipate potential price moves. Something as simple as the percentage average daily range can help you to better see the true risk involved and help to identify which opportunities best fit your risk profile.

There are other key risks and considerations to consider when picking your trading instruments. Another significant factor for a trader to consider is the instrument's liquidity. Liquidity is a measure of the ease with which an asset can be bought or sold, so liquidity risk is the risk that a specific instrument cannot be traded quickly enough to capture a price that you would want. Remember that it is ultimately supply and demand that determines the amount of trading that takes place, and if for some reason the demand for the instrument you have chosen dries up, you may be left holding the bag. When you eventually find someone to sell your illiquid asset to, the price might be significantly different than what you had hoped for or expected.

In extreme cases, which I have personally experienced a few times, a stock can be delisted so you never have an opportunity to sell it at all. For these reasons many traders look for the most liquid instruments to trade.

We have now covered the many different markets and the numerous instruments that you have available to trade. Let's now move on to how you can analyze these instruments to get a better feel for how they fluctuate and reveal opportunities.

CHAPTER 4
ANALYTICAL TECHNIQUES

There are two primary approaches to market analysis in trading: fundamental and technical. Most successful traders ultimately incorporate some combination of the two. The longer your time frame, the more important a role fundamentals will play in your trading, whereas for the shorter-term trader, the technical aspects will be much more important.

If you study investing at an academic level, you will come across the concept of the efficient market hypothesis (EMH). The hypothesis states that market and asset prices at any point in time reflect all available information. As a consequence, one should not be able to make consistent returns greater than the average market returns. Academics claim that successful investors with long, consistent track records are just statistical anomalies.

Personally, after studying and experiencing numerous bubbles and busts, I can't help but feel the EMH does not properly represent reality. Markets fluctuate wildly between over- and under-valuation. Driven by greed, the markets exhibit 'irrational exuberance' and then fall, driven down by the fear of losses. Therein lies the opportunity for traders to make above-average returns—and this is where robust market analysis can (literally) pay dividends.

FOCUSING ON THE FUNDAMENTALS

Fundamental analysis is concerned with the valuation of instruments based on the calculation of the net present value of projected earnings. In other words, it analyzes the financial health of a business within the surrounding economic context. Analysts study financial statements, interview company management, consider macro-economic factors, political cycles, and interest rates; anything that will have an impact on the company's performance. Once a valuation is determined, it is compared to the current share price to establish whether it is currently under- or over-priced. If the market is under-valuing a company's shares, shares can be purchased at a bargain. Having done so, if you wait until the market smartens up and trades at a fair value, you can then cash in your gains.

If only it were that simple.

There are two main challenges with this approach.

1. You need to predict future earnings. Making predictions about the future is easier for some companies than others. These are usually in stable, regulated industries and their shares are also stable and do not offer the level of return that a trader would be interested in. For most companies, their fortunes, and so their valuations, change rapidly, and what was cheap today may be expensive tomorrow.

2. Things are always changing. Technological advances in society have impacted business cycles to the point where we now have new companies experience a major rise, achieve multi-billion-dollar valuations, and then fall in less than a decade. This rapid pace of change can easily make the fundamental analyst's head spin, as can be seen in Figure 4.1.

Figure 4.1: Fast boom and bust in three short years

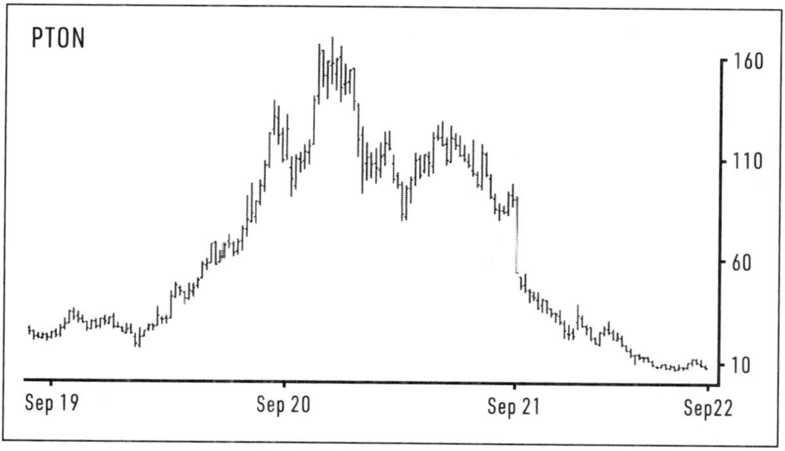

Source: TrendSpider.

Fundamental analysis is the foundation of the investment industry. The investment banking industry has thousands of analysts who provide recommendations from a fundamental perspective. Benjamin Graham and David Dodd's classic book *Security Analysis*, first published in 1934, focuses on fundamentals and has long been considered the bible for serious investors. Graham's most famous student, Warren Buffett, is now one of the richest men in the world, having made his fortune as an investor using the principles of fundamental analysis.

PRICES FLUCTUATE AROUND THE FUNDAMENTAL VALUE

Some pure technical traders pride themselves on not even needing to know the companies they trade, basing their decisions purely on technical signals. But this approach can be reckless, particularly around certain fundamental events like earnings announcements and key economic reports. Fortunately, even if you lean towards the technical side, anyone interested in pursuing a basic understanding of fundamental aspects of trading has access to tons of data through the internet. You also have access to analysts' reports and recommendations. Of course, it is how you use this information that will determine your level of success as a trader.

As a minimum, I recommend knowing at least when a company's earnings announcements will occur, and its ex-dividend date (the cutoff dates for dividend eligibility when buying its shares). There may be significant price adjustments around these times, for which you may want to be out of the market or adjust your signals beforehand.

If earnings from shares in companies were 100% predictable, they would in effect just be like a bond. Their price would be based on a simple formula, and you would know exactly what returns to expect over time. With unpredictable performance and unpredictable earnings, the band of possible valuations of a company widens. What you want to find is a company with relatively predictable earnings or growth opportunities that have not been valued into its current price.

CHAPTER 4

GETTING TECHNICAL

In contrast to fundamental analysis, technical analysis focuses on the use of charts that represent an instrument's price and volume history to predict future price action. At one time, technical analysis was considered the work of the fringe and not taken at all seriously by the mainstream. With the advent of personal computers and the ability to easily prepare historical price charts, the practice has gained a wide audience.

CHART TYPES

Given today's computer power and sophisticated charting programs, you could write volumes on the various styles of chart and indicators that traders are able to draw from. But since we're only summarizing here, a couple of chart styles include the open, high, low, and close (OHLC) and candlestick charts. Indicators include MACD, stochastic, and moving averages.

Each time an instrument is traded, it generates two pieces of data: price and volume. Charting takes this data and represents it visually over a specific period of time. One of the most popular chart formats is the OHLC chart—which in simpler terms is a form of bar chart. Each vertical bar spans the highest and lowest price traded during the time period stated on the corresponding x-axis label. There are then two horizontal ticks extending out from the bar, one on the left side representing the open (the price that the first trade occurred at) and one on the right side representing the close (the price at which the last trade occurred).

Another popular chart type is the candlestick. This is another way of visually displaying the four components, open, high, low, and close. In this case, 'candles' are formed, with the top and bottom of the body of the candle being the open and close prices respectively. Each candle has a wick at both top and bottom, with the end of the top wick marking the high price achieved, and the end of the bottom wick marking the low. Depending on whether the open is higher than the close or vice versa, the candle body is either colored in or not. The resulting chart is then analyzed based on a number of different types and combinations of candles, to help predict moves. Figure 4.2 shows a candlestick representation of QQQ over a six-month period.

Figure 4.2: Candlestick chart

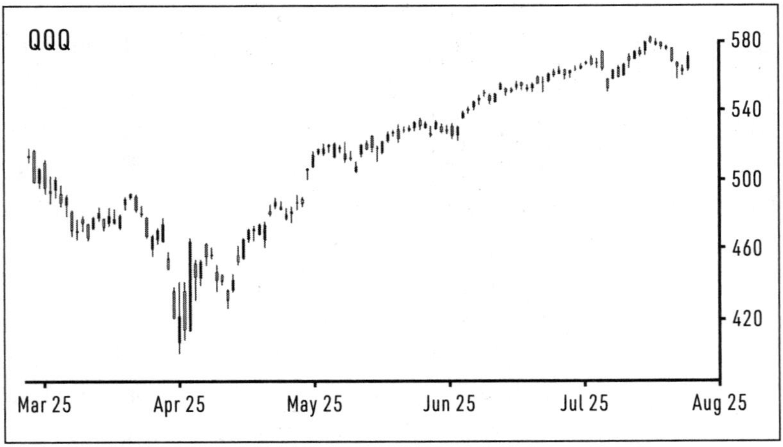

Source: TrendSpider.

Although the OHLC and candlestick charts are the most popular, other chart types you may see include point and figure, Heiken-Ashi, line, and Renko.

Price charts only present the historical prices of trades. Over the years various methodologies and theories have been developed trying to explain what the chart actions mean and how they can be used to predict future price movements. They include indicators, chart patterns, and wave theories, to name a few.

The bible of technical analysis was written by Robert D. Edwards and John Magee, titled *Technical Analysis of Stock Trends*, and was first published in 1948. This followed on the pioneering works of Charles Dow, W.D. Gann, and Richard Wyckoff. Since then, numerous books have been written capturing ideas from basic psychological interpretations to the more obscure ideas involving planetary cycles, sun spots, and Fibonacci ratios. This is one of the reasons that some traders refuse to take technical analysis seriously.

By studying historical prices, with an understanding of the psychological factors around stock trading, technical analysis can prove to be a very powerful tool. The key is to keep it simple. Ultimately what you are trying to do is find an edge or an anomaly to exploit for profit.

Let's review some of the basic concepts. One of the first items to consider is volume.

VOLUME

When a company goes public, the business owners are selling part of the company in the form of shares. The number of shares available is called the outstanding shares. The outstanding shares multiplied by the price of the shares gives us the market capitalization—or the theoretical value of the total company at that time.

Some of the outstanding shares may be held by the original owners, while others may be held by large mutual funds or pension plans that do not actively trade. The remaining shares represent the 'float'—or shares readily available to trade. The volume of shares traded on a given day therefore represents the relative interest in that stock.

For a trade to take place, there needs to be a buyer and a seller. The buyer wants to own the stock, and the seller wants to sell it. The trade takes place at a mutually agreed-upon price, for a specific number of shares.

It is the relationship between price and volume that is used to help forecast prices. Rising prices and rising volume—or declining volume on declining prices—are both bullish combinations (indicative of optimistic market sentiment), while rising prices and falling volume—or rising volume and declining prices—are bearish (suggesting expectations of a downward market trend). Basically, if volume is rising in an up market, it reflects a growing interest in the shares, by those willing to bid up the price.

Likewise, if volume is increasing as prices are dropping, it means traders are willing to take lower prices, as they lose interest in the stock. If volume is declining as prices are rising, it shows that the buying power is drying up, and if volume is declining as prices are dropping then selling pressure is drying up.

You will often see a spike in volume at key turning points. At tops, it represents panic buying from those who have finally gotten the nerve to participate in the great move (that is now over); while at bottoms, it represents sellers who have finally given up their hope of a turnaround or are not able to handle another cent of pain (also called capitulation). Figure 4.3 is a typical example of a chart including volume.

Figure 4.3: Volume chart

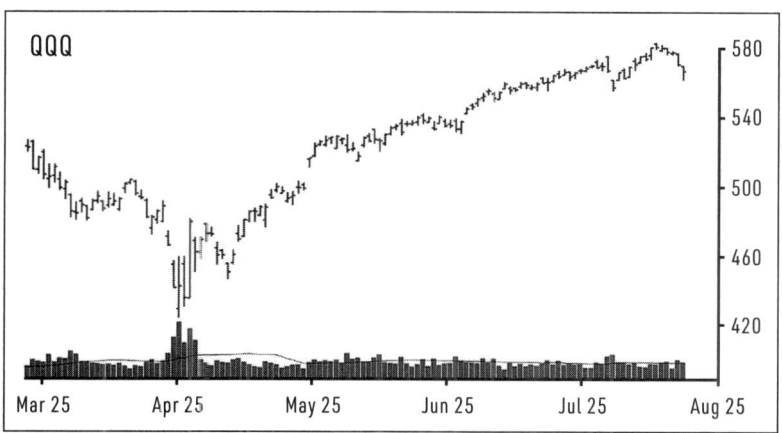

Source: TrendSpider.

TRENDS AND CONSOLIDATIONS (MARKET PHASES)

Newton's first law of motion states that every object in a state of uniform motion tends to remain in that state of motion unless an external force is applied to it. Like physical objects, if you look at stock charts, you will see that this law seems to apply to stock prices as well.

While in motion, stocks are either trending up, trending down, or moving sideways (also known as consolidating). An up-trend is characterized by pricing making higher highs and higher lows, while a down-trend is making lower highs and lower lows. Both trending and sideways price action often stay within distinct channels. Significant changes in trends end at pivot points.

Essentially prices move through various phases that are either trending or consolidating. One of the pioneers of technical analysis was Richard D. Wyckoff, who developed a theory and trading methodology around four phases of the market cycle—accumulation, markup, distribution, and markdown, as Figure 4.4 indicates. Here we see the consolidation phases (accumulation and distribution) interspersed with trending phases (markup and markdown). Traders are fond of the saying "the trend is your friend." A trending stock is an easy way to make money. Traders are looking to identify a trend early and ride it to the end.

Figure 4.4: Wyckoff Market Cycle

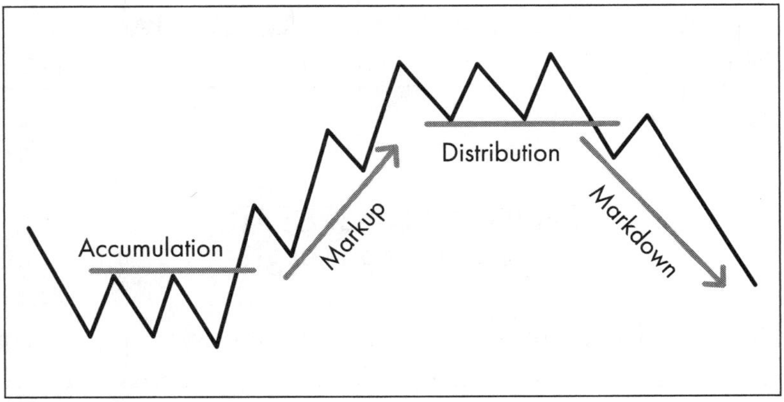

Source: Author.

SUPPORT AND RESISTANCE

Many traders' behavior is influenced by the price they originally paid for their stock. It is also influenced by a number of technical areas that they feel have significant meaning, from simple things like round numbers to more complex and esoteric concepts like Fibonacci ratio retracements. These areas on a chart then become spots where trends are expected to end and pause or change direction.

'Support' refers to an area where prices would be expected to pause in a down-trend as more investors buy or cover their shorts. 'Resistance' is an area where prices would be expected to pause in an up-trend, as investors take profits or initiate short positions. The trend will often continue to break through these zones after the price 'tests' the support or resistance level.

Trend lines can be drawn on charts to highlight these key areas or zones. As prices break through these zones, previous resistance often becomes the new support, and vice versa. As seen in Figure 4.5, traders will then often use these areas to exit their trades, either as profit targets or areas to place their stops. They may also use them as areas to initiate trades if the prices break through.

Figure 4.5: Support and resistance

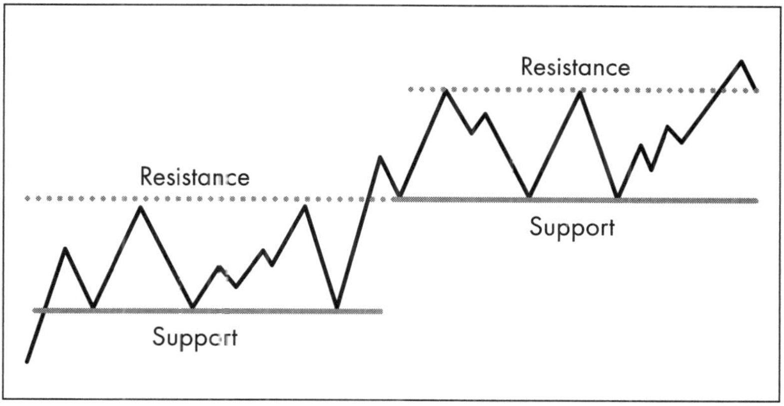

Source: Author.

PATTERNS

If you look at a bar chart with some history, you will start to see more sophisticated patterns than just trend lines and support and resistance areas. These patterns seem to repeat themselves, and technical traders use them to help predict future price behavior. Patterns can be broken into two major classifications: continuation and reversal. Both include patterns for bullish (up-trend) or bearish (down-trend) moves.

Many other books on technical analysis cover patterns in detail, but to give a few examples of both types, continuation patterns include: flags, pennants, triangles, wedges, and gaps. Reversal patterns include: cup and handle, head and shoulder, double tops, triple tops, and rounding bottom.

Is it any wonder that people look at technical traders funny?

INDICATORS

In order to extract more information from a basic chart, technical analysts use data to generate numerous indicators. Indicators themselves cannot forecast prices, but they can give a different perspective on what has happened in the past, and this in turn may indicate what will happen in the future.

By studying the indicators, price, and volume, analysts have more tools to forecast future prices. Combinations of these variables can also be used to develop trading systems. The great thing is that all these patterns, indicators, and systems really do work—at least some of the time.

Indicators can be broken down into numerous categories, for example: price adjustments, moving averages, volatility, momentum, trend, and market strength. There is also a whole group of esoteric indicators, and more are being developed as the search for a better way to predict price continues.

The different categories can also be viewed based on the data that is used to calculate the indicator. Overlay indicators are a group of indicators that are overlaid onto the price chart itself.

Let's look at some of the most prominent types.

Moving average

The most popular type of overlay indicator is the 'moving average.' A simple moving average is calculated by adding up the prices for a specific number of periods and dividing it by the number of periods. The result is the moving average of the price. The price used can be the open, high, low, or close—or a combination of high, low, and close divided by three. A simple moving average (SMA) treats all price points with equal weight.

In order to give more weight to more recent price points, some people use an exponential moving average (EMA). There are also weighted moving averages, triangular moving averages, triple moving averages, and more. This is why there are so many different indicators out there. If analysts can come up with this many ways just to average a few numbers, there is no end to how many ways they can manipulate multiple variables.

Whatever method of moving average is used, when plotted it provides a smoothing out of price. When prices are above the moving average, the stock is in an up-trend, and when the price is below the moving average it is in a down-trend.

There are a few key moving averages that are often used, and you will hear them referenced in the media. The 200-day moving average represents a long-term trend indicator, while the 50-day moving average represents a shorter term. Moving averages are often used to define support and resistance. Traders will also use multiple moving averages on the same chart to help define different time frames. When different moving averages cross each other, they often signal changes in the trend.

> **It's not because two moving averages cross that prices fall— it's because prices fell that the two moving averages cross.**

VWAP (volume-weighted average price)

The VWAP is a moving average that incorporates both price and volume. It calculates the average price over a specific period of time, weighted by the actual volume. Traders use it in a similar way to the regular moving average for trend identification and support and resistance. Given the impact of volume, some feel that it better reflects the true average price.

Bands

Other indicators that are overlaid onto the price chart are known as 'bands.' There are straight bands and volatility bands. Straight bands try to capture the bulk of the price activity. You take a moving average and shift it both up and down by a certain percentage. As prices approach the upper and lower bands, this helps to identify extreme over-bought or over-sold conditions. It also helps to identify dynamic trading channels.

Like straight bands, volatility bands also capture the bulk of the price data. The difference is that instead of being plotted with a fixed percentage above or below the price, they are plotted at a number of standard deviations away from the price. This way they adjust to the volatility of the price. They will tighten as volatility decreases and expand as volatility increases. Traders can use this type of band not only to identify over-bought and over-sold conditions, but also as a basis for volatility-based systems. Stocks often move from low volatility to high, so the bands can help identify these areas before potential large moves. Common types of volatility bands include Bollinger Bands, Keltner Channels, and Donchian Channels.

ADDITIONAL INDICATORS

There are a whole host of additional indicators available to traders on most charting software packages that are normally plotted below the chart. Looking at one common free online charting package, I see there are over 50 indicators to choose from. Traders can also create their own unique indicators, or they can purchase or lease proprietary indicators developed by others.

Initially indicators can help you to get a better perspective of what is happening with the price. Ideally find a few indicators that work for you. It can be easy to become overwhelmed with so many choices, but on closer inspection, indicators can be grouped into classifications or types that provide similar information.

I have seen some traders add so many indicators to their charts that it is a wonder they can make any decisions at all. Using more than a few indicators can lead to them contradicting each other, and the trader becomes paralyzed, not knowing what data to believe. Nonetheless, traders can become obsessed with technical analysis. It can be like trying to find the Holy Grail. They keep adding indicators or combining numerous rules and never get to trading. Don't forget: whether you approach trading from a fundamental or technical perspective (or a combination of both), there is no methodology that can tell you what will happen next in the markets. All you are hoping for is an edge. It is what you do with this information, and how you actually trade, that determines your level of success or failure as a trader.

Here are a few more common indicators used by traders that are included in a number of trading systems—if you use them, use them wisely!

MACD

As you might expect, trend indicators give the most reliable signals when markets are trending. The MACD (moving average convergence/divergence), is one of my favorite indicators. It is derived from two moving averages of the price data. Many traders use a two-moving-average crossover system to trade, and the MACD helps to give a different perspective and offer other signals. The indicator was developed by Gerald Appel in the 1970s and is a very popular indicator available on most charting applications.

The MACD line itself is simply the difference between the two moving averages. With a traditional two-moving-average crossover system, a buy or sell signal would be triggered when the MACD line crosses the zero line. The MACD indicator also includes a moving average of the MACD line, referred to as the MACD signal line. This helps to generate additional trading signals. Some charting packages also provide another visual representation of the indicator, by charting the difference between the MACD line and the MACD signal line as a histogram.

Besides the obvious trading signals created by the crossover of the signal line and the MACD line, the MACD can also be used to identify divergences between price and the MACD line, which helps to identify key changes in the trend. It is also powerful when combined with other indicators that help to identify trending versus non-trending markets.

Range oscillator–stochastic

There are a group of indicators that help to measure a price's momentum, or rate of change, over a period of time. The stochastic indictor falls into this group. It was developed by George C. Lane in the late 1950s. The indicator shows the location of the current close relative to the high-low range set during a given number of days. It is a 'bound' indicator, meaning it moves between 0 and 100.

Like the MACD, there are the obvious buy and sell signals generated, when the indicator falls below 30 and then crosses back above for a buy signal or rises above 70 and then falls back below for a sell signal. Much more powerful signals and interpretations can be derived, however, with divergences.

George Lane ran a company called Investment Educators and has written numerous publications on the use of the stochastic indicator.

Volume–OBV

Volume indicators, predictably enough, use volume as the basis of their calculations. There are many theories about how price and volume interact over time. By creating indicators around volume it may be easier to identify changes that cannot easily be seen by just looking at the volume bars themselves.

On-balance volume (OBV) is one of the more popular volume indicators, developed by Joseph Granville. He wrote about it in his 1963 book *Granville's New Key to Stock Market Profits*. The indicator is a cumulative number, derived by adding volume on up days and subtracting volume on down days.

Divergences between price and the OBV indicator are used to predict changes in trend, or the OBV can be used to confirm the continuation of trends already in place. Figure 4.6 is an example of a chart with price and volume, as well as a few indicators including: moving averages, MACD, and Bollinger Bands.

Figure 4.6: Various indicators—Bollinger Bands, moving averages, MACD and volume

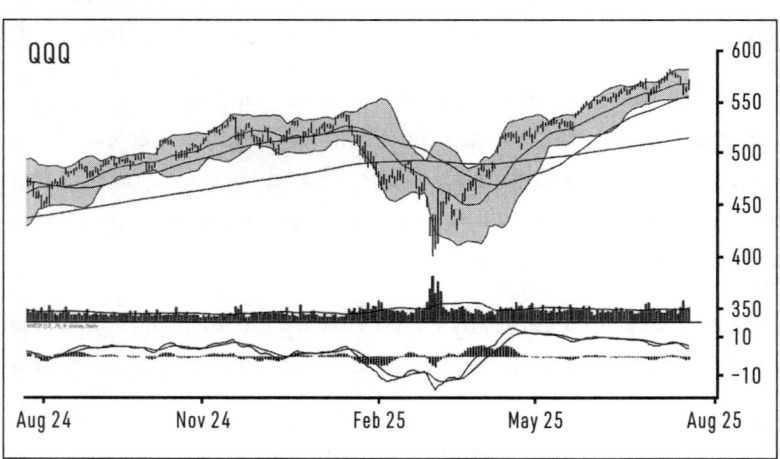

Source: TrendSpider.

CHAPTER 4

WHERE TO FIND CHARTS AND INDICATORS

There are a number of sources you can access to view charts and indicators, ranging from free resources provided with online trading accounts to very expensive applications run by private companies. Depending on the source you use, they may provide either daily data or intra-day data. Daily data would only include one data point (open, high, low, close, and volume) per day and allow you to view charts on a time frame of daily or higher (daily, weekly, monthly, etc.). Intra-day data includes data for all trades that take place and allows you to view charts over any time frame (one minute, five minutes, hourly, etc.).

We have now encountered a number of analytical tools, both fundamental and technical, that traders have at their disposal. Each trader will be drawn to a different combination of these concepts and tools, which will form the basis of a style of trading that will best fit their personality. The more time you spend studying these elements, the better the chance that you will find the methodology that is best suited to you.

The best chance of survival and success is gained by those who study, study, and then study some more. Trading—like any other profession—requires serious dedication and a lot of work in order to become proficient. Unlike other professions, though, if trading is not taken seriously, it comes with a huge risk: the risk of losing whatever capital you dedicate to the business.

The danger at this point is that some people are too lazy to study and too anxious to get trading. They venture down the road of newsletters, blogs, tips, and gurus, then jump straight into trading. As long as you are not trading, newsletters, blogs, tips, and gurus are fine to help with your education. Besides the books that I have already mentioned, the internet is a goldmine of reference materials such as blog posts, podcasts, and Discord servers where successful traders share their outlooks and methodologies for anyone to follow.

> **No indicator or setup is a stand-alone system. You also need rules for money management, entry, exit, and stops.**

Finally, a number of reputable gurus offer training courses and coaching programs to help accelerate you along your learning curve. But don't look to them for the next hot tip or instant success—because dedication, study, and long-term commitment are the keys to successful trading.

SEASONALITY, CYCLES, AND WAVES

I also want to review some popular types of analysis that incorporate elements of both fundamental and technical analysis. The first of these is 'seasonality.' This method seeks to identify and understand underlying fundamental factors that occur on an annual basis and create statistically significant, predictable patterns of behavior.

By enabling you to identify the best times of year to make your moves, these seasonal patterns can give you an edge. For example, the old Wall Street rule "Sell in May and go away" developed to keep investors out of the market during the seasonal slump in the late spring and summer months, where returns tend to be lower. There may be many underlying recurring fundamental factors that create consistent patterns in the overall equity markets. The late spring slump may be from traders leaving the Street for their vacations, for example.

There is also the influence of quarter-end window dressing, tax-loss selling, and holiday shopping (known as the Santa Claus rally). There are also factors that create seasonality at an industry level. For example, the growing season typically creates a summer rally in fertilizer stocks due to the increased demand at this time. Heating season, aka winter, also has an influence on natural gas stocks. The key is to identify seasonal trends that have a firm fundamental foundation, where there is a true cause and effect, not just a coincidence.

Unlike seasonality, which is a cycle that recurs on an annual basis, there are many underlying cycles that occur over shorter or longer periods of time. The repetition of bull and bear cycles, driven from social, economic, political, and investor sentiment, can last for many years at a time, as markets swing from over-bought and over-valued, to over-sold and under-valued. There are also bull and bear cycles for each instrument and sector.

Not all cycles are equal, of course. Some traders believe that there are stock market cycles caused by sunspots and other planetary factors. Others follow Kondratiev Cycles that are believed to last 50 years, presidential cycles that last four years, or lunar cycles that last 28 days. You can, if you wish, look at even smaller time frames and find cycles that last hours or minutes. Like seasonality, the key is to assess and understand the fundamental factors that are behind the cycles—sifting through the distractions to identify genuine cyclical cause and effect—and be sure to stay on the right side of the ones you follow.

In the same line as cycles, a number of wave theories have been developed over the years, the most famous being the Elliott Wave theory developed by R.N. Elliott.

Most people who look at stock charts will say that the price movements remind them of waves. Elliott studied the underlying principles causing these waves and developed analytical methods to help predict future prices. He published his findings in 1938, in a book titled *The Wave Principal*. Robert Prechter, a modern-day follower of Elliott's work, has also published a number of books on the theory, trying to reintroduce traders to these concepts.

Being more of an art than a science, these interpretations are often criticized, since if you ask ten Elliott Wave technicians what will happen, you will often get ten different answers. Having said that, it is still a concept that is very powerful, and there is much value to it that technical traders can use.

THE ELLIOTT WAVE THEORY

Essentially, the Elliott Wave theory states that the underlying crowd psychology in the market moves between optimism and pessimism, in a natural sequence that creates predictable patterns.

Elliott refers to a primary trend move as an 'impulse wave' and the countertrend move as a 'corrective wave' (see Figure 4.7). An impulse wave is broken down into five lower-degree waves—three smaller impulse waves (see waves 1, 3, and 5) interspersed with two smaller corrective waves (2 and 4) creating an overall trend. Following this, the main corrective wave is broken down into three lower-degree waves—two smaller corrective waves (A and C) split by one smaller impulse (B) creating an overall movement against the trend.

What is very interesting is that because of the fractal nature of the markets, the same wave patterns exist when looking at any time frame.

Figure 4.7: Elliott Waves

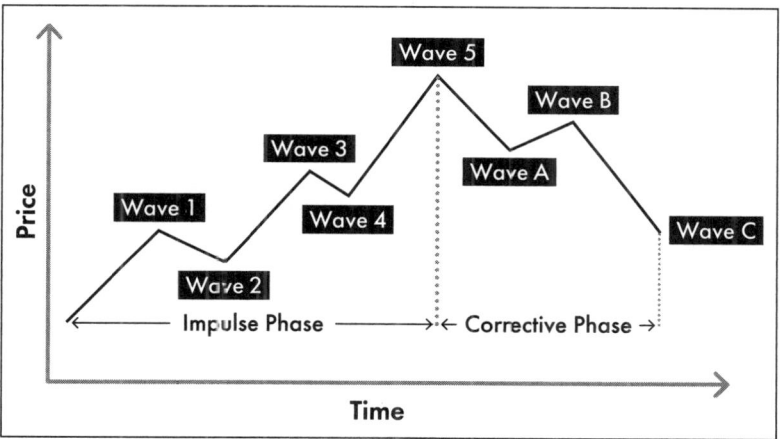

Source: Author.

When you look closely at the wave patterns and understand the emotional reactions to price changes that happen to traders and investors as a group, then the wave patterns make sense.

Let's look at what happens during a change in trend from a down-trend to an up-trend. During the down-trend, there is more selling pressure, which continues to build as more and more people are losing money. At some point, the scared money is shaken out and the bargain hunters start to dabble. At this point a bottom is made, usually with a spike in volume, just when the fear and pain of losing has reached its tipping point. I like to refer to this point as 'point zero'.

At this stage we have a number of investors who have just abandoned ship and are in no mood to jump back in. You also, however, have a group of bargain hunters and technical traders that will purchase. With very little selling pressure left, you see a nice bounce off the bottom. This is Wave 1.

At this point, some investors will want to take profits and some that were not shaken out during the major down-trend may take this opportunity to get out at a better price than the low. This is Wave 2.

Now technically the price action is much more positive; you have the investors who abandoned ship during the down-trend now interested in getting back in again, and finally you also have a larger group of investors who are kicking themselves for missing the nice rally off the bottom. The buying pressure now significantly outweighs the selling pressure, and you see a huge surge in prices. The faster and more significant the move, the more buyers want to jump on the bandwagon. This is Wave 3 and the place where the most money is made in the shortest period of time.

Consequently, as the price moves further you eventually get profit takers and short sellers (who will profit from the price's decline) entering the fray—and so begins Wave 4. This is a period where buyers and sellers tend to be more equally balanced as new buyers enter late in the game and this is offset by profit taking.

Still being in an uptrend, however, at some point the buyers outweigh the sellers. We have a group of buyers that missed Wave 1 and Wave 3 but are determined to get a piece of the action.

These buyers drive the prices to a new high and the final leg of the up-trend—Wave 5—happens.

At this point we have a larger group of buyers sitting on profits, so what follows will be a larger correction, similar to Wave 4.

We start with profit-taking, which creates the first stage of the main corrective wave—Wave A. Since the overall picture is still bullish, we end up with buyers entering again, creating Wave B. This is followed by a final group of sellers, taking profits and creating Wave C. This then takes price to an attractive area, that again starts the impulse wave sequence all over again.

At some point the major trend will shift from positive to negative, and the same wave patterns will appear in reverse. The five-wave impulse sequence will end at the top and a new five-wave impulse sequence will begin on the down-trend. At the absolute top, you have a number of desperate investors who may have missed the ride up but have been sucked into a position at the worst possible time. They jumped on when the opportunity cost of missing the move reached a point where they could no longer stand aside.

At this point, you also have a number of lucky investors that want to take profits, as well as short sellers who want to take a first stab by taking advantage of the overvalued situation. This creates the Wave 1 moving down.

The first move down gives profits to the short sellers, after which the few traders on the long side come back into the game by buying the correction, against the main trend. This creates Wave 2. At this point, the balance has shifted from positive to negative, as the first move down has shaken the confidence of the long traders, who now fear the top has been made. Selling pressure begins to mount. The short sellers who missed the first move down jump on board with a vengeance and Wave 3 begins and soon builds momentum.

Wave 4 begins once the selling pressure climaxes, and the shorts start to increase their profit-taking. The struggle is fairly matched between the bears and bulls, creating a counter-trend rally. Finally, Wave 5 takes prices to a new low, as we have the final weak hands selling their holdings and the final group of shorts, who eventually get the nerve to short the end of the trend.

As you can see there are numerous ways to not only display a chart of price and volume, but also endless analytical techniques to add different perspectives. The next step is to review the various trading styles.

CHAPTER 5
TRADING STYLES

MANY NEW TRADERS jump into trading with very little thought as to what style would best fit their unique situation. They are exposed to trading tales on social media and are attracted to the methods based more on unrealistic expectations than on what will work best for them. Ideally before developing the more detailed strategy, you should review the various styles and do a self-assessment to see what best aligns with you.

As discussed in Chapter 2, there are a number of factors involved in a trader's decision on what style of trading they will lean towards. The key components include: the amount of time they can commit to trading, the amount of time they have a trade on (i.e., how long they're willing to hold the instrument before selling), their risk tolerance, expected profits, financial goals, their capital available, their education and knowledge base, and their emotional resilience.

Finding the right style to begin with can save a trader a lot of pain and suffering. I have seen many individuals with low risk tolerance and a full-time job try to day trade high-leverage instruments. This does not end well. Financial losses, emotional distress, and destroyed confidence can end a trader's career prematurely. A style that you are truly aligned to will help set you on the right path right from the start. Even existing traders that are struggling often find significant improvement with a re-alignment.

Alignment is not a 'one and done' exercise. As traders continue to evolve and mature and their lifestyles change over time, reviewing their current style and making changes may be what is needed to improve their trading performance.

> **Learning to trade, like learning most creative endeavors, often begins by copying the works of the masters.**

Of course, before you can reflect on the aforementioned factors to identify the trading style that best aligns with your personality, you will need to know what styles exist to choose from. Let's consider the main options now.

TIME-BASED STYLES

The following four styles are grouped according to the length of time that a trader is willing to hold their positions and the expected price movement they are trying to capture.

CHAPTER 5

SCALPING

Of all traders, scalpers have a trade on for the least amount of time, often for only a matter of seconds. They are trying to profit from *very* small price movements. This is a high-volume, low-profit-per-trade style of trading, where technical analysis would be the major analytic technique used. Scalpers must be very focused and need to be able to make quick decisions and execution. I consider scalping to be high risk, given the number of trades involved and precision required.

DAY TRADING

Day traders, as the name suggests, initiate and exit trades within the same day. They will start and end the day with no trades on, unwilling to expose themselves to the risk of holding a position overnight. Like scalping, this style requires a high volume of trades, with relatively lower profits each time. Day traders are trying to capture more profit per trade than scalpers, but this is limited by whatever daily moves are available. Most are technical traders, with little emphasis on fundamental analysis. I consider day trading to be moderate-to-high risk, mainly due to the frequency of trades.

SWING TRADING

Swing trading attempts to profit from short-term trends, with a holding period covering multiple days. Swing traders do not have to make as many trades as scalpers or day traders and are focused on capturing larger moves. Swing traders also do not need to sit in front of the computer screen to identify and track their trades, although many still do. This style of trading is mostly traded from a technical perspective, but it can also factor in fundamentals to help identify trading candidates. Risk is lower than day trading, but this style requires patience and the ability to hold positions overnight.

POSITION TRADING

Position trading is a style where the trader attempts to capture longer-term trends, often holding positions for weeks or months. Position traders are much more reliant on fundamental factors and less on technical.

PRICE-ACTION STYLES

The next styles are differentiated by the type of price action that the traders are trying to capture, either going with the flow or fighting the herd instinct.

BREAKOUT TRADING

Breakout trading involves capitalizing on price movements as they break through significant support or resistance levels.

TREND TRADING

Trend trading involves following the prevailing price trend, such as using the 'buy the dip' strategy, buying pullbacks in the trend or continuation moves.

MOMENTUM

Momentum trading is a style that attempts to enter a trade in the direction of the current, often fast-moving, trend and price action instead of trying to anticipate where the action will be; like jumping onto a moving train, these traders go to where the action is *now*. Characterized by high volatility, high volume, and fast-moving prices. The trades are often short-term and high risk, requiring quick decisions and close monitoring.

COUNTER-TREND TRADING (REVERSALS)

Counter-trend trading is a style that attempts to profit from changes in the direction of the prevailing trend retracements that run counter to the main trend.

RANGE/CHANNEL TRADING

Range trading is a style that focuses on markets that are not trending, but trading within horizontal support and resistance levels. Traders identify overbought or oversold conditions using oscillators, selling the top of the range (resistance) and buying the bottom of the range (support).

Channel trading is similar but trading within a channel formed by trendlines when market are trending.

REGRESSION TO THE MEAN TRADING

Regression to the mean trading is when traders assume that price action will revert back to its historical mean (average) price after extreme moves. Also called 'mean reversion trading,' it see traders trading against the current trend after large price moves.

APPLICATION STYLES

Application styles refer to how strategies are actually implemented or executed.

DISCRETIONARY TRADING

Discretionary trading involves the trader personally implementing and executing each trading decision. They call the shots for each trade. Discretionary trading is when a trader may change their interpretation of any signal or chart formation based on the current environment. They may still have a specific set of rules that guide their trading but will only take trades at their own discretion. Not all moving average crossovers signal a true change in trend or that an oversold stochastic is ready for a bounce. Other factors that may not be easily put into system rules or are learned after years of experience allow traders to enhance their returns by ignoring signals that they feel are not likely to work out. The danger of course is that discretionary traders can fall victim to the trap of following emotional decisions rather than educated ones.

MECHANICAL OR SYSTEMATIC TRADING

Contrary to discretionary trading, mechanical or systematic trading is a style in which a trader follows his set of rules exactly, often through an automatic system linked directly to their broker. The rules are usually created and tested against historical data, through rigorous back testing. All signals and trades are taken to ensure the integrity of the system parameters. Many traders develop and test their own systems. There are also many software programs with these applications, and services are available to develop programs with your trading ideas. Finally, there are many black box systems available to purchase or lease from system developers.

The advantage of systematic trading is that it theoretically takes the emotion out of the equation. It is often emotional reactions that kill traders. This might sound ideal, but the hard part is resisting any emotional reactions that will prevent you from following the system and its signals. The disadvantage is that during times when the strategy is not working out you may experience drawdowns that discretionary traders could avoid. It also requires a strategy that can be programmed specifically, leaving no room for experience to alter. This style requires a certain skill set that many traders lack and a reduction in flexibility many are not willing to accept.

STICKING TO THE PLAN

All traders need to have a detailed trading plan that provides clear trading rules, and that plan begins by knowing what style of trader they want to be. It is best for first-time novice traders to try and follow the rules religiously. I say *try*, as this is nearly impossible. Over time you will get a better handle on your emotions. You will also gain the experience to start deviating from the plan. Many traders, after gaining experience over many years and many market cycles, will have developed multiple styles that adjust with the market environment. They have trend-following methods when the markets are trending and counter-trend methods when they are retracing, for example. Traders also often move from day trading in their youth to position traders in later years.

> **Knowing how to trade often means knowing when not to trade.**

PUTTING IT ALL TOGETHER

In the last two chapters we have covered a number of different analytical techniques and trading styles. You can understand now just how many ways there are to trade, and it is likely that you will feel yourself being drawn to a combination of the techniques and styles that best fit your personality.

When considering your personal approach, there are a few critical factors that will influence your decision: the amount of time you can dedicate to your trading is a big one as it will influence not only whether you are a day trader or position trader, but also how much time you have to dedicate to analysis. You will also be drawn toward certain analytical methods, based on factors such as your background, education, and philosophy.

I also want to remind you that the instruments you decide to trade, the leverage you are willing to assume, and the style of trading itself determine the level of risk you are taking on. Like any new skill, it is always better to walk before you run, and this is especially true where there is a significant risk. With trading, even with proper money management rules in your trading plan, if you start by trading higher-leveraged instruments, you run a huge risk of losing your capital. It is all too easy to break your own rules, and this is especially true for novice traders.

You can now start to see just how interrelated all the various components are that we have covered. The objective is to make sure that these components are compatible with your overall objectives in order to ensure the most effective alignment.

Once you have a handle on your style, the next step is to develop your overall business plan, which includes your detailed trading plan. These components will be covered in the next two chapters. Let's begin with the next chapter, which emphasizes the importance of viewing your trading as a business.

CHAPTER 6
DEVELOPING A BUSINESS PLAN

ONE OF THE great things about trading is that it is a very simple business model. There are essentially no barriers to entry, little capital requirement, and no employees to deal with. Unfortunately, being such a simple business to get into means that many traders jump in without the proper analysis, planning, or documentation.

In simple terms, a business plan is a formal statement or document that outlines your goals and how you plan on achieving them. Most traders spend all their time developing a trading plan, which *is* a key component of the business plan, but there is so much more. The primary objective of a business plan is to bring clarity and consistency to your trading business, helping to minimize impulsive decisions and provide a solid foundation to build from. Imagine if you had to seek funding from an investor or bank in order to get your trading business off the ground. The business plan they would expect to see is exactly what every trader should develop.

A well-documented business plan is one of the most critical steps a trader can take to help ensure their long-term success. What I suggest in this chapter are the bare minimum requirements. Your plan is a living document that will evolve over time. Initially you should err on the side of adding too much information. Committing your plan to writing is very powerful.

There are several key components to consider when creating your business plan.

Many of the areas we have reviewed in previous chapters—such as your trading style, analysis methodology, and instruments to trade—will go into your business plan too. But let's dig deeper and expand the content.

The first part of your business plan should focus on you as a trader. The major components will define your personal 'trader profile.' The five major components are closely interrelated and must be balanced to fit your personality and resources. These are:

1. Why am I trading?

2. Trading capital and goals

3. Risk tolerance

4. Time commitment

5. Trading style and strategy

These are foundational to the type of business you will be running. Let's begin with these five major components. Think about them by answering the following questions:

CHAPTER 6

1. WHY AM I TRADING?

Success in any endeavor often hinges on *why* we are doing it in the first place. Many traders are initially attracted to trading for the money, with no real passion or understanding of what trading really entails. Once they have some experience and realize what is required, they either quit or get serious. If you have got this far and are still serious about trading as a business, the chances are you will be motivated by something more than just money. Of course you *are* still in it for the money, but other driving factors could include: the independence and flexibility of running your own business, being accountable for your own results, the intellectual challenge, and the personal growth that comes from confronting the psychological issues that arise as you evolve. Having a strong 'why' can help you stay committed when exposed to the inevitable challenges that will come your way.

> **If you are not treating your trading as a business then you are probably treating it like an expensive hobby.**

2. TRADING CAPITAL AND GOALS

How much capital do you want to commit to the business and what are your profit goals?

Let's face it, it takes money to make money, and if you are serious about making money trading it is important to set realistic goals regarding the amount of capital required and the expected returns. Unfortunately, the industry is full of people making unrealistic claims about the riches that can easily be made in the markets. Traders then approach the business with goals that just do not match reality.

My advice is to start with an amount of capital that you are comfortable risking, spend as much time as needed to learn the fundamentals of trading (and more specifically your personal methods) and adjust it as needed. Your initial goal should be to protect your capital and not lose money. Only after you are comfortable with your methodology and making consistent profits should you think about adding to your capital base or withdrawing funds on a regular basis.

You also need to have a realistic budget for operational expenses. Computer systems, software, data, internet and education materials are some of the fixed and ongoing expenses that need to be budgeted for.

A big mistake that new traders make is to assume that they will hit the ground running, make consistent profits, and be able to withdraw funds on a regular basis to pay their living expenses.

Many new traders' first goal is to make money rather than to develop solid business and trading plans. Spend the time on the plans and the money will follow.

CHAPTER 6

I have seen traders think they can make a six-figure living trading with $10,000 of capital. Two things usually happen here, they either quickly realize that this is impossible and add to their capital base, or they assume enormous risks and are wiped out after a few trades. Some of the most successful traders in the world are quite happy with 20% in annual returns and I can never quite understand why a novice believes they will be able to pull off triple-digit returns on a regular basis.

Their logic goes something like this: if I aim to make $100,000 per year and there are approximately 250 trading days, then I only need to make $400 per day to achieve this. With $10,000, I can trade 400 shares of a $25 stock and only need to capture a $1 per day move to reach my goal.

It sounds easy when you frame it this way, which is one of the reasons why so many traders get sold on books, courses, seminars, and gurus that promise millions. However, another way to look at these figures is as a 4% daily return, a 20% weekly return, and an annual return of 1,000%. Of course, there are individuals that do make huge gains, but there are also individuals who win the lottery or make it big at the casino, and these feats are usually a one-time event and are almost impossible to duplicate.

New traders should initially plan to break even at best for some period and set 10–20% goals in the long run. This might come as a wakeup call, but it is a lot better to start with realistic goals and build your business slowly than to quit your day job on your first day of trading. Those that set unrealistic goals tend to get frustrated and discouraged quickly and either quit when funds are needed and not materializing or assume huge risks and get wiped out.

3. RISK TOLERANCE

Ultimately, trading involves risk. We buy and sell financial instruments, and whenever we have a position on we are exposed to risk. Risk to our hard-earned dollars. Your risk profile is a key component in deciding the trading style and specific strategy that you plan on following. How well can you handle a significant loss? Where is your 'ability to sleep' point?

4. TIME COMMITMENT

This is another area where new traders have some very unrealistic expectations. They think they can look at a few charts or get a couple of recommendations from their subscriptions, place a trade, make some money, and repeat. How much time does that take? Well, like any other business, there is a lot more involved.

You need to dedicate time to your learning plan, the evaluation of potential trades, placing trades, monitoring trades, tracking trades, evaluating closed trades, and accounting for trades. Of course, your style of trading will also have an impact on the amount of time required. If you plan on being a day trader, you will obviously need a lot more time than if you are a position trader. Day trading would be a full-time business, whereas other forms of trading can be done on a part-time basis.

Successful traders are usually obsessed with their trading and have no issue dedicating time and effort towards their business. They are passionate and driven. Those that lack the drive to dedicate the time are usually in the wrong business and soon see their capital dwindle.

Don't be fooled by the promises of quick money. Dedicating the necessary time is critical to your trading success.

5. TRADING STYLE AND STRATEGY

By now you will have an idea of what trading style you intend to implement. Remember, the critical point here is to have a style that fits your personality, but you also need to be able to dedicate the time and capital needed to make it work. Most new traders do not understand the many different approaches to trading that are possible, assuming they just buy an instrument and then sell when it gains value.

However, because you have an education plan, you will study famous traders and will add the knowledge gained to the core concepts we've already covered to see that there are many approaches that can be pursued. Find the approach that you are comfortable with and document the main concepts for this part of your business plan. Try to create an elevator pitch about what you do as a trader and your trading strategy. What is your trading edge?

The next section of your business plan should include:

6. Work instructions (process)

7. Physical and psychological management

8. Education plan

9. Trading plan

6. WORK INSTRUCTIONS (PROCESS)

Once you have documented your trading strategy you can focus on creating a work instruction of your daily, weekly, monthly, and annual routines. This will include the various steps you will take to run your business. Having a regular routine and process to follow will help keep you focused and committed to your overall plan. What is your pre-trading process, when do you review trades, when do you identify new opportunities?

7. PHYSICAL AND PSYCHOLOGICAL MANAGEMENT

What routines do you follow to maintain your physical and psychological well-being, such as exercise, meditation, and diet? What techniques do you incorporate to help manage your psychological and emotional issues? What will you do for emotional support?

I have outlined that the major risk involved in trading is found in the emotional state of the trader. In this part of the plan, you should develop an approach to maintaining and dealing with your ongoing physical and psychological well-being. This could include a regular fitness schedule, massage, journaling, and therapy, as an example.

You should also commit to gauging your ongoing emotional state and be prepared for times when you may need to back away from trading altogether. We will cover more detailed plans in Chapter 9.

8. EDUCATION PLAN

As covered in Chapter 2, by now you should have a detailed education plan that you would include within your business plan. Most successful traders are passionate about trading and never stop learning about the craft. Your plan should cover all the different aspects of the trading business, in an order that makes the most sense to you, to help get you up and running and develop those areas that you need, within your budget and time available.

CHAPTER 6

9. TRADING PLAN

The final component of your business plan is your detailed trading plan.

The next chapter focuses on the trading plan, which forms a key part of the overall business plan. Here we will include your specific detailed trading strategy and money-management rules.

CHAPTER 7
DEVELOPING A DETAILED TRADING PLAN

WE HAVE NOW documented the major components of your business plan, and it is time to drill down into your detailed trading plan. This is where we get into the daily standard operating procedures that you will put in place to implement your trading strategy. The more detailed this plan is, the easier it will be to follow, and it will help you to avoid the emotional traps that threaten your business's success.

The most critical point to make about the trading plan is that *you* must develop the discipline to follow it religiously. This is where most traders fail. One of the main reasons for having a trading plan is to eliminate all possible emotional aspects. This is a business in which giving in to your emotions is the quickest path to ruin.

Since most people do not have the willpower necessary to be successful traders, it is a good idea to find a method of forcing yourself to stay with your plan. You can hire a trading coach, join a trading group or social network, or start a blog, for example. Anything that keeps you accountable to your trading plan and encourages the discipline required to see it through. Like a smoker who tells their friends they are going to quit, success is made much more likely by committing to a group that holds you accountable to your goal.

Your detailed trading plan should encompass:

1. **Markets and instruments**:

   What market will you trade in: NYSE, Nasdaq, CME, or somewhere else? What will you trade: stocks, options, futures, or other instruments? How will you screen?

2. **Broker/trading platforms/tools**:

   What broker will you use? What does their platform look like? What other tools and services are you using?

3. **Trade setup and execution**:

   Detailed rules around your chosen trading strategy. How will you identify setups, enter, exit, and re-enter a trade? What stop-loss (more on these soon) and take-profit levels will you use? What types of orders will you place?

4. **Money/risk management**:

   This section defines the percentage of capital you will invest in each trade. How many positions do you trade at once? What percentage of risk do you take on with each trade? How do you determine position sizing? What are your capital allocation, diversification, and stop-trading rules?

5. **Trading journals (financial and non-financial):**
   What journaling will you do to monitor your emotions and capture lessons learned from successes and failures? Do you do mindfulness or stream-of-consciousness journaling?

Trading plans are where many traders spend the majority of their time studying, as they lay out actual trading rules that include all of the key components of a trading strategy.

Some traders focus on one strategy or setup and become experts at finding it in the market and trading it. The limitation here is that it may only fit one part of a market cycle. Others have multiple setups they trade, each fitting a certain cycle in the market, so that they are always able to find opportunities.

Let's consider each of the key components that your plan should include in more detail.

1. MARKETS AND INSTRUMENTS

This section outlines the markets and the specific instruments you plan on trading. Why have you chosen these specific instruments? Is the list static or do you adjust it over time? How do you determine which instruments to trade? Do you scan from a universe of instruments and narrow it down, and if so, what are your criteria? Or perhaps you are just trading one specific instrument like an S&P 500 ETF. Whatever you have chosen to trade, provide the criteria and logic behind your choice here.

When it comes to screening, there are many tools available to help identify opportunities that may fit your particular parameters. Do you have key setups or indicators that you are screening to narrow down your trades?

The decision to trade certain instruments is also closely related to what level of risk you are willing to assume. Volatility, margin requirements, and leverage used should be included here as well.

2. BROKER/TRADING PLATFORMS/TOOLS

Trading is a business, and like any business the objective is to maximize your profits. For most traders, one of the biggest operating costs is commissions. Luckily, commission costs have fallen dramatically over the last few decades, with major consolidations in the brokerage industry and the technological advances with the internet.

Historically, commission costs were a major barrier to entry for traders with small amounts of capital. Even successful small traders gave most of their gains back to their brokers in the form of commissions. There are still full-service brokers, but traders also have the option to trade with discount brokers, as well as deep-discount brokers (where, depending on the size of the trade, these costs can be eliminated completely).

Of course, when choosing your broker, cost is not the only consideration. Like any other service you pay for, the needs of each trader may be different and must be considered. Some key considerations are: the trader's level of trading experience, the size of their trading account, their comfort level with technology, and their trading style.

Here are the key things to consider when choosing your broker.

CHAPTER 7

EXPERIENCE WITH TRADING

Some traders like the comfort of using a full-service broker, so they can have a voice of reason in case they are tempted to make some dangerous emotional decisions. The danger here is that the trader comes to use the broker as a crutch, relying on them for trading decisions and advice. Make sure you continue to develop your own style and independence.

SIZE OF ACCOUNT

If you are starting with a small amount of capital, you probably cannot afford the luxury of a full-service broker. The commission cost as a percentage of the trade value will make earning a profit nearly impossible. The advent of online deep-discount brokerage has been the only reason small-cap traders stand any chance at all. With a large account, of course, money talks. You can not only negotiate a better deal with a full-service broker, but in some cases, avoid commissions altogether.

STYLE OF TRADING

If you plan on being a scalper or day trader, you will have no option but to trade online. The instantaneous executions and feedback are critical to your success. If, on the other hand, you are going to be a position trader, you may be able to function with a full-service broker.

With advances in technology, online deep-discount brokerage firms have been able to provide exceptional service at costs that are significantly lower than their full-service counterparts and discount broker competitors. No matter what you decide, make sure you are getting the best value for your commission dollars. I have seen traders who are more than able to handle online trading continue to use their traditional brokerage methods and failing to adjust with the times. They are essentially throwing dollars away for no good reason, lowering their returns, and seriously jeopardizing their chances of success.

MARGIN ACCOUNTS

When opening a brokerage account, you must decide whether or not you need a margin account. A margin account is an account where the broker will loan you money to purchase securities. Essentially, it is like a line of credit, with the cash and securities in the account acting as collateral against the loan. It is also required if you are going to be shorting securities, since when you are short, there is theoretically unlimited risk, which the broker wants to be able to cover from a loan, if necessary. You will also require a margin account if you trade futures, forex, or sell options. Trading these instruments or strategies can expose you to significant risk and should be aligned to your risk profile.

The amount of margin that a broker can provide is tightly regulated and can change depending on the market environment. Security regulators in the past have reduced or eliminated the amount of margin that can be provided.

ADDING BROKERS TO YOUR PLAN

Add the details of the broker or brokers you have chosen to trade with to your trading plan. Include all the details of your accounts and access. Explain the reasoning behind your choice. What criteria did you use to determine which broker to use? Do you have a Plan

B in case of an emergency (if a power outage halts trading with the platform you have chosen, for example). How do you use your broker's platform?

TECH SPECS

What other tools including software, hardware, websites, blogs, Discord servers, and podcasts do you use and incorporate into your trading process?

Depending on the trading style you choose, you may have very different computer and software requirements. A longer-term position trader may be able to get by with just a basic computer with an internet connection. Traders who will be developing and back testing their own systems will require significantly more software and computing power. While day traders and scalpers may require the most expensive live data feeds and computer systems, longer-term investors may not. Don't forget to factor in backup plans, in case of internet failure or system crashes.

Provide the details and logic for each and what specific value they provide.

RISK CONTROLS

Things happen when you least expect them, and having money at risk with no ability to manage can be stressful and potentially financially devastating. Are you prepared for this? What plans do you have in case the internet goes down? What if your power goes out? Do you have a way to access your account by phone? Do you have your account numbers and passwords readily available?

3. TRADE SETUP AND EXECUTION

This is where you document the detailed trading strategy rules that you have developed, back tested, and experienced. It will include how you identify setups, how you enter, exit and re-enter a trade, how you establish stop-loss and take-profit levels, and what types of orders you will use. Even discretionary traders need a set of rules that they can follow depending on the various potential outcomes they encounter.

The overall strategy is the combination of rules that you are looking for that help define your strategy's edge. It can be as simple as a favorite chart pattern or as complex as you want, with a combination of indicators, price action, and volume action. Many traders become confused about what it means to have an edge—a necessary requirement for a trader's success. Put simply, an edge has two components. The first is a strategy that gives you a positive expectation of profit over time. Based on the detailed trading plan that you are documenting here, you should know that you can expect to generate a positive return. Most traders spend a majority of their time on this aspect of their edge, continuously refining and testing to ensure a positive expectancy. What they often miss is the second component of their edge, which is their ability to trade the strategy consistently and accurately. (We will talk further about this component of your edge in Chapter 10.)

> **Patience is not about waiting until you are in the mood to trade, it is about waiting until the market is in the mood to be traded.**

CHAPTER 7

WHAT TIME FRAME ARE YOU TRADING?

As discussed earlier, in the Elliott Wave section, the fractal nature of markets allows you to trade various methods at different time frames. Day traders may trade a five-minute chart, whereas a position trader may trade with weekly charts. If you look at both of these charts without the time and price reference displayed, it may be difficult to tell which is which. This means that there are a number of setups that appear and can be traded in any time frame. Also, although you may be trading off a specific time frame, many traders take various time frame perspectives into account, to help identify potential trading candidates or to help improve the odds of a setup working when there are multiple confluences across time frames.

Now it is time to document the detailed trading rules you plan on following. These rules will have been established to fit your personality and trading style, then possibly back tested to ensure their historical success. Back testing can be done manually or performed automatically with computer programs. You may also use rules established by others, by purchasing their systems that have already been tested. Back testing your complete set of rules will give you a good idea of win/loss ratios, expected drawdowns, strings of gains or losses, and expected returns. Back testing is important to provide you with the confidence you need to carry on trading the rules during periods of drawdown. Back testing is a significant component of strategy development for automated trading systems, but discretionary traders can also back test as they develop and revise their strategies. Not all traders do back testing—some instead develop their strategies around proven, high-probability setups others have tested, or they 'future test' with smaller size to gain confidence.

THE BIG PICTURE

Before we get into the specific rules of entering a position, it is important to have a method of looking at the bigger picture, in order to gauge how the overall market is doing, so you can put today into its proper perspective. Usually this would involve looking at a longer time frame than you are trading and using tools such as wave theory and your usual indicators. Sometimes you may see a great trade on a lower time frame that will not look so good when viewed from a different perspective.

PROFITING FROM DOWNTRENDS

Before we get into how to enter a position, I want to review the concept of short selling in the stock market.

As a trader, our goal is to capture profits from any movement in the market. There are opportunities to capture either upward or downward moves. Most people have no problem with the idea of buying low and selling high. This is the way our brains are wired and how most traders operate. But there is also a way to sell high and buy low, known as short selling.

With short selling, you are making the same transactions, only in reverse order. This is accomplished behind the scenes through your broker, borrowing shares from someone who owns them and who lends them temporarily to you, for a moderate fee.

You will need to replace those shares at some time, but in the meantime, you can sell them to someone else at the current market price and, as long as you can buy them back at a lower price and return them within the loan period, you can make some money from a down-trend in the stock.

CHAPTER 7

ENTRIES AND EXITS

Entries—initial

The first rule you need to have in your plan is a rule for entering a position. You are trying to enter at a price as close to an expected move as possible, with minimum downside risk and maximum upside potential. You want to establish some logic for the entry price that provides an edge observed over a period of time and which is expected to continue.

Price, patterns, indicators, seasonality, and wave analysis are just some of the methods that traders use to initiate a position. Often this will include a setup and a trigger.

An example could be that you are trading a breakout strategy, so you want to buy when the price has crossed above a previous resistance level.

Exit—prevent loss

Whenever you have a position on, you must always have a price at which point you know the trade is no longer working according to your plan, or at which point the maximum loss you have established initially has been reached. You must have a rule to get out. This could be based on a specific pattern, a significant price point on the chart being breached, a fixed dollar value, or a percentage away from your cost. This rule is critical in order to follow one of the cardinal rules of trading: cut losses short.

Exit rules can be automated in many cases with the use of stop orders. From time to time, you may find your stops have caused you to exit a position prematurely but still feel there is potential for the move. Which brings us to...

Entries—re-entry

You will also need a set of rules relating to re-entry. I have seen so many traders get stopped out initially and go looking for another candidate, only to see their original trade work out almost exactly as expected, and they have missed it completely. By having a set of rules for re-entry, you will avoid this frustration. It is not uncommon for false moves against the expected move to shake traders out.

Entries—add on

Some traders like to test the water with an initial position and then add on to it as the move progresses in their favor. This minimizes the loss if the original move does not pan out as expected. There are also traders who like to add to positions that do not originally work out as long as they are still within their risk parameters and setup criteria. We never know exactly where price is going to change direction. Most books on trading advise against adding to a losing position, yet I have seen many successful traders who break this rule as part of their trading style. The key is to ensure that it fits with your overall risk management plan.

There are many money management strategies for building positions on and off, and if you are following this style of trading, you will need rules for these as well.

Exit—profit-taking

What goes up must go down, and vice versa. You must have a dynamic strategy to identify where you will take a profit. This can be set as a target, a significant price point, or at a trailing price—either a fixed dollar value or percentage—away from the best price.

Trend traders with a longer time frame usually leave more room in their exit rules and are less likely to set a specific profit target. Their approach is to ride the trend for as long as it continues to develop and not to presume that they know when it will end. Shorter-term traders, like day and swing traders, usually have specific measured moves that they are trying to capture and will have specific price objectives as their exits.

ORDER TYPES

When transacting in the markets, there are a number of different order types that you can use. The different types can be used to help minimize the risks of bad entries and exits, protect profits, minimize losses, and allow for a more sophisticated overall trading strategy. I outline the major order types here. For your trading plan you should explain what order types you will be using, and when, as you execute your strategy.

Market order

The market order is an order that is transacted immediately on being received at the prevailing market price at that time. This is used when you want to enter into a position immediately, with no conditions at all. In theory, you should buy or sell at the current market price, but there is no guarantee. In the case of an illiquid stock, or a fast-moving market, you may end up with a price significantly different than you thought you would get.

Limit order

A limit order is an order to buy or sell at a specific price or better only. In the case of the market order just provided, where price is fast-moving, you can use a limit order to prevent paying more than you are willing to. For example, if the stock is currently trading at $100, a limit order could be placed to buy with a limit of $101. Likewise, if you owned the same shares and placed a limit order to sell at a limit price of $110, you would never receive less than this amount per share.

Unfortunately, there is no guarantee that the order will be filled. If you are buying the limit price, it can be placed either above or below the current market price. You would place it above the current price if you want a market order, but do not want to pay more than a certain value. This could be useful in a fast-moving market. If the limit price is below the current market, then you will be filled only at that price or better. This could be used for people trying to buy at or near specific support levels, as an example.

Likewise, for selling, you can place the limit price above or below the current market price. If the limit is below the current price, you are willing to sell at the current market value.

If the limit sell price is above the current market price, then essentially you have established a target price that you want to receive. This also can be dangerous, if the price never quite reaches this price and turns around.

Stop order

A stop order is executed as soon as a transaction occurs at your 'stop price.' You can set a stop order to buy at a certain price in an upward trend or to sell at your stop price when the price is declining.

Since the order then becomes a market order, there is no guarantee that you will get the *exact* price you were expecting. When buying the stop price, it would be above the current price—this order is also referred to as a buy-stop order (or a stop-loss order if you are buying to cover a short position).

When selling, the stop price would be below the current price, and this order is also referred to as a stop-loss order (or a stop-sell order if initiating a short position).

The stop-loss is what you hear about most often with this type of order. It is used as a price at which you want to sell a long position.

You can combine a stop order and a limit order, where once the stop price is hit, instead of becoming a market order, it becomes a limit order.

These are three of the more common order types and should handle most traders' requirements. There may be others available from the brokerage you use, some of which you may find useful.

When placing an order, you are also given the option of the time frame that you want the order to be good for; either for the day or until cancelled. Also, for thinly traded securities, you may wish to use an 'all or none' order, which requires the whole order to be filled at once or else the order is not filled at all. This prevents only a small part of the order being filled, or partial fills being spread over a period of time, with the possibility of you incurring multiple commission charges and a wide range of prices.

4. MONEY/RISK MANAGEMENT

Some will say that the money management component of your trading plan is the most important factor in determining your success as a trader. Your ability to keep your losses small and avoid significant drawdowns in your equity is *critical*. After all, you need capital to trade, and a large loss can have a devastating impact on a trader's ability to recover—both financially and psychologically.

When setting your financial goals, you must keep in mind the concept of 'risk of ruin.' Risk of ruin looks at the probability of losing capital to a point where it becomes impossible to recover. Trading, after all, is the investment of money into an event with an uncertain outcome, with the hope of earning additional money and the risk of losing it all. There are two components that determine your risk of ruin:

1. The probability of failure.

2. The portion of your total capital that you wager.

The higher the probability of failure and the higher the proportion of your capital you wager, the higher the risk of ruin. But don't panic, in a moment I will lay out two key money management rules to help prevent this loss from occurring.

Learn to love the small losses. They sure beat the large ones.

As a trader, you must always walk a line between wanting to capitalize on a great trade and limiting your exposure, so that you are never positioned to take a catastrophic loss. Not only do you need to set rules for each individual position, you also need to consider the risk of the total portfolio of trades that you have on at any one time. Although it might always feel like you have too small a position on with your winners and too large a position on for your losers, it is important to have a consistent approach.

RULE ONE: POSITION SIZING BASED ON THE PERCENTAGE OF CAPITAL RISKED PER TRADE

This first rule is to help determine your position size for any single trade. The key variable here is what percentage of your total portfolio you are willing to risk. As you would expect, the less you risk, the lower the probability that you will experience a large loss.

Most traders recommend risking no more than 2% of your trading capital in one trade, with lower amounts being common practice with large professional portfolio managers. You can calculate the maximum position size that you can trade using the 2% rule. The other factors are your portfolio size and the potential risk on the trade, which we calculate based on the difference between your entry price and your initial stop (because a stop will prevent you from losing more than a limited portion of your capital).

Let's assume you have a trading account worth $100,000 and find an attractive stock trading at $50. You want to buy in and intend to do so with an initial stop of $48.50 (so you will risk $1.50 of your invested capital per share). To calculate the maximum position size, you would divide the maximum risk of $2,000 (2% of $100,000), by the $1.50 risk, to get 1,333 shares. Table 7.1 shows the various position sizes for different stop levels on a position. The more you are risking on a position, the smaller the number of shares you would be able to buy.

Table 7.1: Various position sizes for different stop risk levels

Total Portfolio	$100,000
Risk %	2.00%
Risk $	$2,000
Stock Price	$50.00

Stop Risk	# of Shares	Total Investment
$0.25	8,000	$400,000
$0.50	4,000	$200,000
$0.75	2,667	$133,333
$1.00	2,000	**$100,000**
$1.25	1,600	$80,000
$1.50	1,333	$66,667
$1.75	1,143	$57,143
$2.00	1,000	$50,000
$2.25	889	$44,444
$2.50	800	$40,000
$2.75	727	$36,364
$3.00	667	$33,333
$3.25	615	$30,769
$3.50	571	$28,571
$3.75	533	$26,667
$4.00	500	$25,000
$4.25	471	$23,529
$4.50	444	$22,222
$4.75	421	$21,053
$5.00	400	$20,000

When you look at this closely, you will see that this is great in theory, but there is still much more risk involved in practice. If you purchase the 1,333 shares, you will have invested $66,667—a significant percentage of your total portfolio—with the false comfort that the most you could lose on the trade is $2,000. But markets can be unpredictable. So, what happens if the market gaps significantly, breaking through your stop of $48.50 to open at $42.50? If you are then stopped out, you have just lost $10,000, a far cry from your 2% comfort level.

What this tells us is that risk is not as simple to determine as we would like. Remember that the true expected risk is the expected size of the loss multiplied by the probability of the loss occurring. In this case, the expected size of the loss is $1.50, which is still uncertain, and the probability of the loss can only be estimated, based on a number of factors including the volatility of the instrument that is being traded, your trading system (especially if holding overnight), and the market environment. Since you can never know with 100% certainty what the true risk is, it is always better to err on the side of caution and reduce the size when possible, especially for the novice trader.

Of course, there are many other approaches to position sizing that a trader can incorporate into their trading plan. Another method is the 'Kelly Criterion,' a formula that helps determine what percentage of your portfolio should be used in each trade to maximize your long-term growth based on the historical wins and losses of you and your system. This method will once again give you a percentage of your account that you should invest in any one position; but is also theoretical and does not guarantee that no catastrophic loss will occur—which ultimately is the goal of any good money management system.

A simpler method is to divide your portfolio into a fixed number of parts and limit your exposure on any one trade to the value of one part. Of course, the larger the size of your portfolio, the more parts you can have, but a minimum of five would provide a great starting point to ensure a safe level of diversification. You can then focus your efforts on proper stop placement, which is the second key component of money management.

RULE TWO: STOP PLACEMENT

The second money management rule focuses on the type of stops you will use and where to place them.

We calculated your position sizing based on the risk between your entry price and your exit price if your trade goes against you (i.e., your stop). The assumption is that this will be the maximum loss that you will incur. It assumes that if the trade moves against you, you will exit the position if it hits this price—and that it will not blow past this price before an exit can be made.

Essentially there are two types of stops that can be used to ensure this happens: an actual stop order and a mental stop. Believe it or not, many traders shy away from using an actual stop order. They use excuses like "other traders hunt stop levels to pick up cheap stock" or they "feel more comfortable monitoring the position" in case they need to change the stop based on price behavior.

One of the cardinal rules of stops is that you should *never* move them farther away than originally decided when the trade was entered. Set your maximum-loss point and *stick to it*.

What often happens is that traders watch the move going against them and convince themselves to ignore the stop level when reached, since surely it is now oversold (i.e., its rapid price decline means that it is temporarily 'cheap') and is due for a rally. This oversold position often becomes *more* oversold, the exit gets ignored, and losses accumulate. Holding the position becomes too painful, and exits are made losing much more than originally decided.

It does not take too many trades like this before it becomes difficult to recoup your losses, and you approach risk of ruin. The sooner a trader understands the mathematics of losses and the ability to recover, the sooner they will commit to never letting this happen again. The best way to avoid this and get into the habit of respecting your exit price is to place the stop order.

This also applies to profitable trades going in your favor. This is *your* money and should be protected in case of an adverse move when you are not watching. Having a trailing stop—one that moves with the market price as it rises—in place that gets adjusted in your favor over time is a great practice.

There are many ways to determine where to place your stops. Some traders use key technical locations that, if hit, would negate the premise on which they placed the trade in the first place. Others use a fixed percentage or dollar amount that equates to the risk they are willing to take.

You may recall from Chapter 2 that "only trade with money you can afford to lose" is one of the most common pieces of advice that you will read in trading books, but it is one that I have a hard time endorsing. I have seen too many traders take it to heart, living and dying by this principle.

They save up some money that they can afford to lose, and then they lose it. They then save up some more money that they can afford to lose. Guess what? They go ahead and lose that too. This goes on and on. This is not trading, it is throwing your money away.

When trading, your money is your most critical asset and must be protected at all times.

The sooner you focus on that, the sooner your skills will improve.

5. TRADING JOURNALS (FINANCIAL AND NON-FINANCIAL)

Traders are often advised to maintain journals to help with their business, but there is much confusion as to what this entails. When I refer to journaling, I break it into two very different types: financial and non-financial.

'Financial journaling' refers to the process of capturing the financial data of your actual and proposed trading.

This is used for pre- and post-trade analysis, in order to monitor performance and help identify your strategy's strengths and weaknesses. The information you capture and analyze can be used to find areas to avoid as well as areas to focus on to enhance performance.

Like with any business, in trading it is critical to capture and analyze data, not only from an accounting perspective to be able to complete tax returns, but also to gain perspective on how you are really doing.

Some traders track their trades manually in a worksheet, while others rely on data from their brokers and import them into software to carry out more detailed analysis. There are numerous software programs available to help with this. You want to capture all the data around a trade: date, time, volume, entry price, exit price, and so on. These can be used to measure profitability, win/loss ratios, average gain, average loss, etc. Many journal writers also include defined setups, and copies of charts before and after trades. These can help you better understand what is working, what is not working, and where you should focus efforts for improvement.

'Non-financial' journaling captures and addresses the *emotional* aspects of your trading. Given the importance of managing your emotional state in this business, and building emotional resilience over time, this is a critical component to success. Unfortunately, it is an area that many traders shy away from and do not take seriously. I cannot emphasize enough that this type of journaling can make the difference between success and failure, between mediocre results and consistent profitability. Successful traders are willing to confront their demons, limiting beliefs, and psychological issues. Journaling offers you a way to identify and resolve these impediments, *if you* are willing to do the work.

There are a number of different approaches and tools available for this type of journaling. Your first priority is to become more aware of your emotional state. As humans we are continuously bombarded by thoughts, feelings, and emotions that we normally just accept with little critical analysis, not realizing the impact they have on our behavior. To rectify this situation, begin to capture your emotional state in your financial journal—before, during, and after each trade. Are you feeling excited, scared, anxious, or greedy? Maybe you are suffering from 'FOMO' (Fear Of Missing Out)? By capturing these feelings, you force yourself to become more aware of *why* you are doing what you are doing. You begin to see the impact that these emotions have on your results.

Another form of non-financial journaling is 'stream of consciousness' journaling. Like the name implies, you just write whatever comes to your mind, often filling a few pages each day. Many traders do this first thing upon waking to clear their heads, and many of those are shocked to learn how self-critical they are. They start to see patterns that can then be challenged and replaced with more positive and constructive thoughts and self-talk.

You can also do more traditional journaling, in which you dig deep into specific issues or capture what you are grateful for, for example.

All of these forms of journaling are valuable tools on your trader's journey. They can offer a very powerful means of insight and help accelerate your progress.

YOUR DAILY ROUTINE

It is much easier to maintain the discipline needed to successfully trade if you develop a consistent approach with a regular daily routine. Trading itself is only one part of the trading business, and those that ignore the administrative and ongoing learning aspects of that business are more likely to fail.

Although each trader must develop their own work plan, built around their own life and their style of trading (the day trader's schedule will be different from the longer-term position trader's schedule), there are fundamental principles that, if included and followed religiously, will give you the best odds of success.

Here is an example of a routine that includes the key components, as a guide:

Let's assume you are a part-time swing trader with a full-time job where you have some time in the morning to manage your trades and dedicate time after the close to carry out additional tasks, and let's start with the beginning of the day before the opening bell. You should have any changes to existing positions or additional trade opportunities identified from the previous day. Depending on your strategy, you may enter your trades before the open or be ready to trade once the bell rings. For example, some traders like to wait until the open to see how things unfold and what impact this may have on their plans for the day. Either way, during trading hours if possible, you can monitor your positions and make whatever decisions and orders you deem necessary. If you do not have time, then you would rely on the daily charts and orders to manage your trade automatically.

Between today's close and tomorrow's opening bell, there are a number of activities that need to be carried out. Some traders like to do these things immediately at the close, while others like to take a break and tackle them early in the morning before the markets open.

Firstly, you should update your trading records by making sure your day's trading activities are entered in your trading worksheet (if you want to track your own trades), or you can review your electronic broker statements for accuracy and completeness.

You would review the closed trades from the day, new positions that were entered and held, as well as your previous holdings that did not change. This is to determine what changes to your strategy and orders need to be made for the next day. This may include changing stops, revising profit targets, and figuring out where to add. Depending on the current market environment, you may also make adjustments to the levels of risk you are willing to take and either reduce some size or add more.

You should now be in a position to see if there is any room left in your trading capital to add other trades on, based on your money management rules and the current market environment.

You would then create a list of potential trade setups for the next day. This may include signals from trading systems, markets scans, or just some old-fashioned chart reviews. Based on the room left, you should narrow down the list to the best-looking candidates and document the strategy for each, preparing your orders for the next day. You are now ready for the next trading day.

Besides the daily routine, traders should also develop a regular weekly or monthly plan to review all trades for that period. This will form part of your education and strategy development plans. You should run an analysis of your trades and update your key trading statistics. This is another opportunity to reflect on your closed trades, after some time has transpired. The objective is to prepare your trades, execute your trades, assess the outcomes of your trades, and make whatever adjustments you deem beneficial for your continued growth as a trader.

It is amazing when you view closed trades from a longer time perspective how much more educational it can be. Based on the outcomes, you may revise your trading rules to improve your performance. Keeping accurate and detailed records is a form of journaling that is invaluable to the trader who is willing to record and analyze consistently as part of their routine.

Like your business plan, your trading plan is a living document that at any point in time captures your processes, rules, and reasoning behind the components that make up your overall strategy. Also like your other plans, you will continue to monitor and revise it as you mature, which may well cause you to make adjustments. Committing the plan to a formal document and reviewing it on a regular basis will help to keep you aligned and on top of your game.

As you gain more experience, expand your education, and the wider context of your life changes, you may find that your style will also evolve. You will therefore need to change your business and trading plans accordingly.

CHAPTER 7

When it comes to trading plans there are as many approaches as there are traders. Although all components of your trading plan are critical, the main focus revolves around the setup and execution component. In the next chapter let's look at some examples for your reference.

CHAPTER 8
EXAMPLES OF TRADING PLANS—SETUPS AND EXECUTIONS

WE HAVE NOW covered most of the key components that need to be considered for your trading business. In this chapter I will demonstrate some simple examples of trading setups and executions, the most detailed element of your trading plan. These will cover a number of different approaches. It is not my intent to convince you of a best approach to use, as I hope that the importance of finding a style that fits your personality is clear by now.

To generate the best returns, your plan should also fit within the current market environment or cycle. As we have seen in Chapter 4, there are many methods to help understand and identify where we are in a cycle. The Elliott Wave theory is one, but you may also be drawn to Wyckoff Phases or Stan Weinstein Stage Analysis, depending on where your further education leads you.

By showing a number of approaches, I want to demonstrate how easy it is to develop a system and tweak it, as you go along on your trading quest. Think of creating a new recipe. You start with basic ingredients and combine them to develop a new dish. Once you have created something, you can then make adjustments to suit your preferences.

The plans I present are simple for a reason. Although many traders start with sophisticated systems, with multiple indicators and complex rules, most successful trading systems eventually evolve into a few basic rules. The examples are meant to give you an introduction to the various key strategies that many traders gravitate toward. As you find an area that you are interested in, further research will uncover volumes of material to help you fine-tune your own strategies and approach.

> **Successful traders develop strategies over years and adapt to changing market conditions as they arise. There is no best strategy.**

These examples are also shown for illustration purposes only and are not meant to be examples of profitable edges. They can be used as a starting point to test and develop trading plans around.

For the purpose of demonstrating the plans, I will be using the futures market and stock market to trade in. Most of these systems, however, can be used for any tradable instruments.

1. FADING THE GAP

Day traders love to trade S&P futures contracts, because of liquidity, the tight bid-ask spread (the difference between the highest price a buyer will pay and the lowest price a seller will accept), and high leverage.

THE SETUP

In this setup, you would 'fade' an opening gap, essentially taking a position that is opposite to the direction of the initial move. Like most good setups, you will find that this can be hard to do, as it goes against the crowd. In this case, the markets have gapped up or down, indicating an initial imbalance of buy and sell orders and causing a significant change from the previous day's close. The underlying reason for taking this trade is that under certain circumstances it is common for the gap to be filled.

In this setup, we want to sell a gap up or buy a gap down, on the open.

Table 8.1: Key considerations for fading the gap

What time frame are you trading?	One-to-five-minute chart.
Select your market and instruments	Futures contract S&P 500.
The big picture	I will also use a 30-minute chart to gauge the longer-term trend of the market and try to identify the type of gap. Ideally, I want an exhaustion gap (which signals a trend is breaking).
Entries—initial	Buy gap down on the open, or sell a gap up on the open.
Entries—re-entry	Not applicable.
Entries—add on	Not applicable.
Exit—prevent loss	Initial stop: 25% of the average daily range for the last ten days.
Exit—profit taking	Trailing stop, plus profit-taking when the gap is filled.

Figure 8.1: Fade the gap

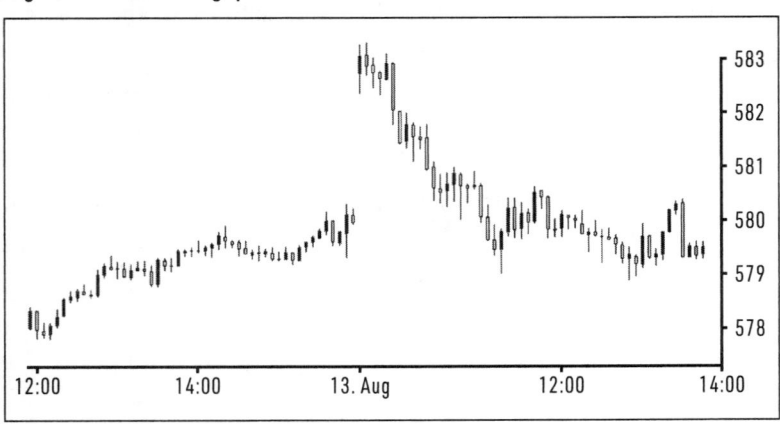

Source: TrendSpider.

CHAPTER 8

2. HIGH MOMENTUM

As a trader, money is made when things are moving. You can either look for high-volatility price moves that fluctuate up and down or price moves that are nicely trending. High-momentum stocks fit the latter category. These are usually stocks in successful companies that are favorites on Wall Street, with good fundamentals, institutional ownership, and lots of public interest.

THE SETUP

Nothing goes straight up. The pattern we will be looking for is the 'bull flag.' A bull flag is a pause in an upward price trajectory that happens when traders sell to take profits. The goal is to jump on for the next rally.

Table 8.2: Key considerations for high momentum

What time frame are you trading?	Daily.
Select your market and instruments	Specific stocks would be identified by scanning for new highs. In order to qualify as a high-momentum stock, by definition it would be making new highs. I will then monitor for profit-taking and the bull flag pattern to emerge.
The big picture	This pattern works out best when the markets are positive.
Entries—initial	Entry at the high of the previous bar, as the bull flag is developing. I may also consider a more aggressive entry at the perceived bottom of the bull flag, at the high of a key reversal day.
Entries—re-entry	If stopped out, I may have been premature on the bottom of the flag and want to continue to monitor and re-enter.

Entries—add on	I can add my second position at the top of the bull flag.
Exit—prevent loss	Stop-loss is set at the low of the flag.
Exit—profit taking	Move stop to breakeven once the high of the flag is taken out. Trailing stop from this point on.

Figure 8.2: High momentum—bull flag

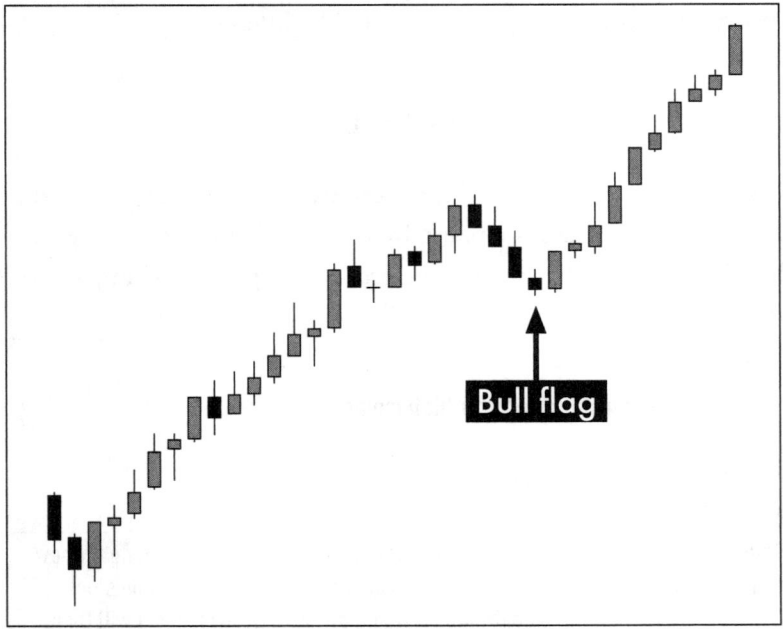

Source: Author.

3. BURSTING BUBBLES

In this strategy, I am looking for short candidates—outrageously over-valued stocks that have experienced parabolic price moves and are running out of steam.

A trader's propensity to try and pick tops and bottoms is a common emotional trap. However, there is a time and place for it.

I am talking about companies that have become not only the darlings of Wall Street but have gathered such a following that they become ridiculously priced—way outside of the normal bounds of valuation. When these bubbles burst, there are often significant declines in a short period of time.

Of course, like fading gaps, we are definitely trading against the herd here.

THE SETUP

Shorting the first sign of weakness after a parabolic price move in stocks that have seen significant price appreciation over long periods of time. Bubbles do not get created overnight, so patience is the key here. I am looking for MACD divergence and/or a head-and-shoulders pattern (reversal patterns) to identify the top.

Table 8.3: Key considerations for bursting bubbles

What time frame are you trading?	Daily and weekly charts are used to identify the setup, but I will be trading the daily chart.
Select your market and instruments	Specific stocks would be identified by scanning for new highs and significant price appreciation in the last 12 months. The high-flying stocks are usually well known and easily identified from various sources. I can either short the actual stock or participate with put options. Some of the candidates that I have been trading using the high-momentum setup may eventually become good candidates for this swing position bubble burst setup.
The big picture	Although bubbles can burst at any time, the best performance would be during an overall market decline. In some cases, the bubble bursting is what precipitates the market decline.

Entries—initial	After a new high is reached with MACD divergence, I wait for the first wave down and a bounce that does not take out the previous high.
Entries—re-entry	If I take initial profits from the second move down, I should be ready to re-enter this position on a bounce.
Entries—add on	Ideally, I want to ride this move down and be able to add to my position as the profits start to accumulate.
Exit—prevent loss	The initial stop would be at the previous high. (This may also be an opportunity to stop and reverse my position, as these are usually high-momentum stocks that may be reaching for a new high.)
Exit—profit taking	These setups can offer a huge return to those who are willing and able to be patient. There is often a nice move down from the bounce, where initial profits can be taken, but I need to be ready to re-enter.

Figure 8.3: Bursting bubbles

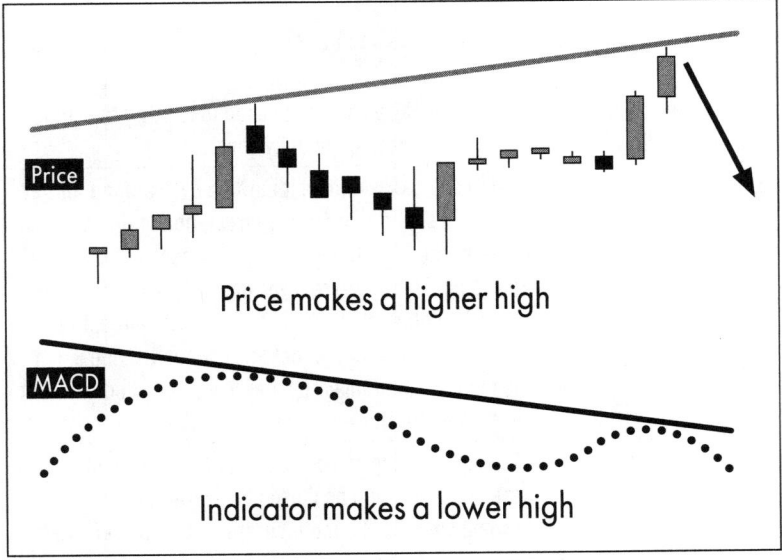

Source: Author.

CHAPTER 8

4. REVERSAL PATTERN

There are a number of setups based on classic chart patterns to choose from and specialize in.

THE SETUP

Two classic reversal patterns are the double top and double bottom. The double top is when the price makes a new high, followed by profit-taking and then the price rallies to the previous high. The double bottom is when the price makes a new low and then buying takes the price off the bottom, which is followed by selling to take it back to the previous low. We will buy the second bottom or short the second top.

Table 8.4: Key considerations for reversal pattern

What time frame are you trading?	Daily chart.
Select your market and instruments	I will scan my usual suspects, visually looking for the setup to occur.
The big picture	Looking for overbought conditions for double top and oversold conditions for double bottoms.
Entries—initial	For double bottoms, I buy when the price hits the previous low. For double tops, I short the previous high. I can also consider a stop-and-reverse order if either stop is hit, as it may signal a continuation of the previous trend.
Entries—re-entry	If I am stopped out of the double top short and it ends up being a false breakout, I may want to consider re-entering short as it dips back below the previous high. If I get stopped out of the double bottom and it ends up being a false breakdown, I may want to re-enter the trade long, as it bounces back up above the previous bottom.

Entries—add on	If this is a significant reversal, I may be entering a position at the best possible time and want to add on to the position as profits build.
Exit—prevent loss	The stops can be placed just above the previous high for the double top and just below the previous bottom for the double bottom.
Exit—profit taking	Profit can originally be taken as prices reach the level of the previous profit-taking for the double top and the short-covering or buying-pivot point for the double bottom.

Figure 8.4: Classic chart patterns—double bottom

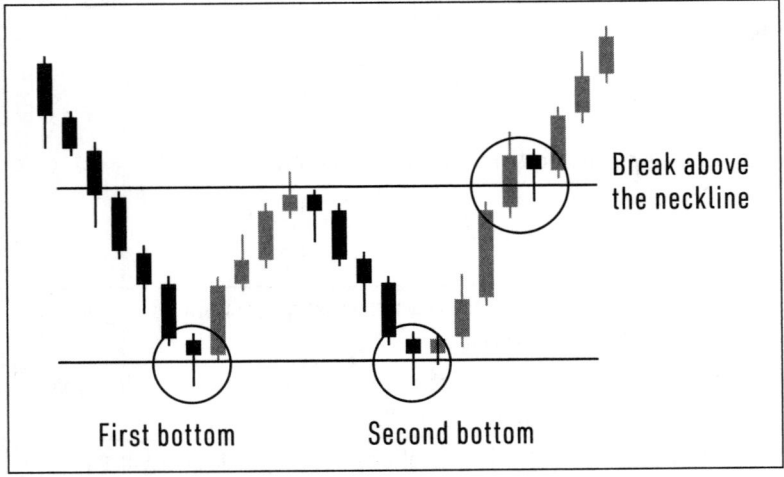

Source: Author.

CHAPTER 8

5. UNDERVALUED ASSETS

There is an old Wall Street saying that posits the best time to buy is when "there is blood in the streets." This refers to those times of critical under-valuation that happen during major bear markets or significant market collapses, when all stocks are pulled down, no matter what their true value.

This is when true contrarians thrive, building positions in under-valued companies. It is at the market extremes that the majority of investors are wrong, and so the trader attempting this setup requires a strong constitution to fight the masses. Knowing when the down move is over is key.

"Catching falling knives" is another common expression, this one describing unsuccessful traders' attempts to pick at the market bottom, only to see new lows. The key is to add technical indicators to the setup, which will help identify when the drop is over.

THE SETUP

Buying the first sign of strength after a collapse, in a stock that has seen significant price erosion over a long period of time or after a significant rapid collapse. We are looking for MACD divergence and/or a head-and-shoulders pattern, or a key reversal day (in which the price reaches a new low before reversing to close above the previous day's close), with a spike in volume, to identify the turning point. We also want to add a fundamental filter in order to find the most successful companies.

Table 8.5: Key considerations for undervalued assets

What time frame are you trading?	Daily and weekly charts are used to identify the setup, but I will be trading the daily chart.
Select your market and instruments	Specific stocks of fundamentally strong companies would be identified by scanning for key ratios, like low P/E ratios, low debt, and strong earnings growth. I will be monitoring these during the bear market or collapse for specific technical patterns and signals.
The big picture	I want to see the turnaround setup in the overall market to show a true end of the trend or collapse.
Entries—initial	After a new low is reached with MACD divergence, I will wait for the first wave up and some sell-off, that does not take out the previous low. I will also take a key reversal day, with a spike in volume.
Entries—re-entry	If I get stopped out, I should be ready to re-enter after new lows are reached and the setup repeats itself.
Entries—add on	Ideally, I want to ride this move up and be able to add to my position as the profits start to accumulate.
Exit—prevent loss	The initial stop would be at the previous low. (This may also be an opportunity to stop and reverse my position, as I may be premature in the entry and further lows may be coming.)
Exit—profit taking	These setups can offer a huge return to those that are willing and able to be patient. There is often a nice move up from the bounce, where initial profits can be taken, but I need to be ready to re-enter.

Figure 8.5: Bargains after a collapse

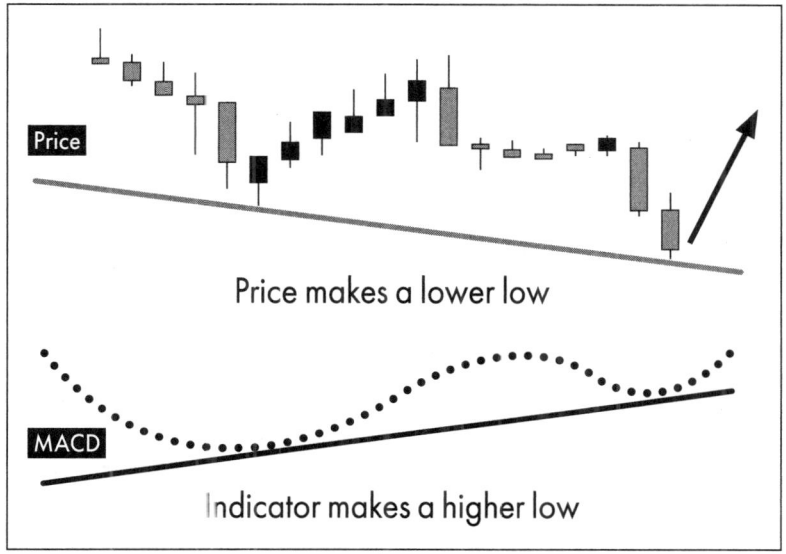

Source: Author.

6. TRADING RANGE

Since prices usually only trend about 30% of the time, unless you are really patient you run the risk of giving back profits during the 70% of the time that markets are range-bound. There are a number of trading setups that traders use during these quiet times.

THE SETUP

Buying the bottom of the channel and selling the top of the channel, using a momentum indicator like the stochastic indicator and price. This can also be used for significant support and resistance levels that have not necessarily formed a channel.

Table 8.6: Key considerations for trading range

What time frame are you trading?	Daily.
Select your market and instruments	The best approach is to scan charts for range-bound patterns.
The big picture	There are usually lots of candidates, if the overall markets are also range-bound. I will look for setups after periods of significant trends. The key is to identify a range-bound market as soon as possible. The longer a market is range-bound, the higher the probability that it will eventually either break down or break out of the range. (For Elliot Wave practitioners, look for Wave 4s for great setup opportunities.)
Entries—initial	Once the range parameters are identified, I can enter long at the low of the range or short the top of the range. I can also use the stochastic indicator to help identify oversold or overbought conditions.
Entries—re-entry	If stopped out, it may be from a false breakout or breakdown, and I may then have a second opportunity to get back on, as it re-enters the channels and continues to trade within the range.
Entries—add on	Depending on the size of the range, I may be able to add on once the move is underway.
Exit—prevent loss	Initial stops would be placed just outside the range.
Exit—profit taking	Profits will be taken once the price reaches the other end of the range.

Figure 8.6: Trading range example

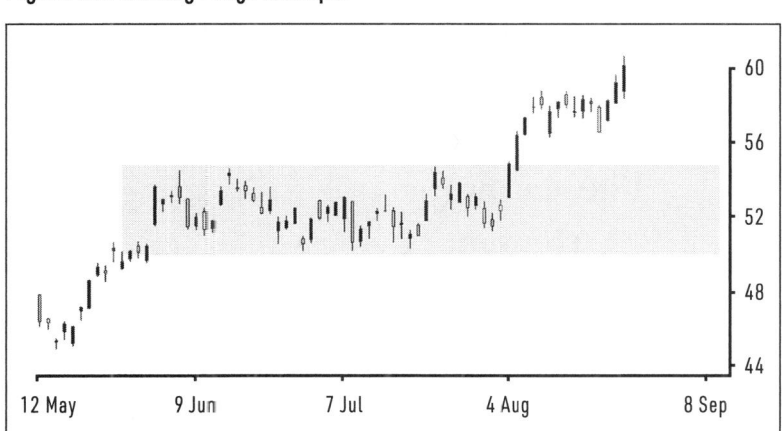

Source: TrendSpider.

Since markets spend so much time range-bound, there are lots of opportunities for traders with this setup. It follows that once the markets break out of their ranges, there are great opportunities to capitalize on the trending markets that follow.

As you can see, there are a number of different setups and strategies available for traders to choose from and specialize in. You will also notice that different strategies work best for different market environments. As you gain more experience, you can add more setups to your trading plan and move from one environment to another, with a strategy to make money on a continuous basis.

> **Many new traders ask for the secret formula to trading success expecting an easy road to riches. The secret formula for trading is the same as for any other profession: passion, commitment, perseverance, and hard work.**

I hope these examples have provided you with an idea of just how many different opportunities there are available for your trading business. Even with a great trading plan in place, the next challenge is to trade it consistently. In the next chapter we address some of the common psychological issues traders encounter as they begin to trade their plan—issues that are often the biggest obstacle to a trader's ability to be consistently profitable.

CHAPTER 9

TRADING PSYCHOLOGY I— OBSTACLES ALONG THE WAY

OVER THE LONG term, a trader's success is dependent on them having an edge. That may seem like common knowledge, but many struggle with what it means and how to achieve it.

I see a trader's edge as having two key components:

The first component is a trading strategy that, when implemented over time, has a positive mathematical expectancy. You can establish this expectancy by multiplying the percentage of your trades that make a profit by the average gain of those trades, then adding the percentage of trades that make a loss multiplied by the average loss of *those* trades. If the result is a positive number, then you have a positive expectancy.

Think of yourself like a casino in which the many games and rules they have in place guarantee them a positive outcome over time. Ideally you have developed a strategy and either back tested or paper traded it enough to make you confident that this component of the edge is solid.

The second component is your psychological edge—your ability to trade your strategy as intended. You must develop the resilience and discipline to trade your strategy consistently without succumbing to the emotional trading mistakes that most traders make.

> **Successful traders do not beat the market, they beat themselves.**

Of course, you won't know whether you have this resilience until you can recognize the emotional trading mistakes to avoid.

EMOTIONAL TRADING MISTAKES

Emotional trading mistakes have ended the careers of countless traders. Trading the markets is an opportunity for self-evaluation and self-improvement, but until you get a handle on it, it can cost you a lot of money and pain.

Emotional management is critical to your success. It never ceases to amaze me how readily traders attempt to justify their emotional behavior from an intellectual perspective—behavior that is costing them money and causing them pain. A good rule of thumb is: if you are losing money, take a close look at your behavior, because this may need adjusting before your strategy does.

Whenever you have a trade on, it is like having an ongoing psychotherapy session. You will constantly be learning new things about yourself. You can either take the opportunity to learn, and change your behavior to improve your trading results, or you can ignore the lessons the market provides and carry on making the same mistakes until your patience and capital are gone (or you admit to yourself that you are not willing or able to deal with your limitations, and leave the business).

The best way to begin to tackle your emotional management is to develop a trading plan with an edge. Once you have done this, you know statistically that if you trade the plan exactly over time you will have a positive outcome.

What tends to happen, however, is that traders encounter markets that make it hard for them to pull the trigger when they get a signal, or they pull the trigger prematurely. This then results in performance that is nowhere near what is expected from the plan.

Most novice traders take a system with positive expectations and turn it into negative results. Their emotional responses to the actions in the market are so powerful that they change rules that are fundamental to their success.

> **The market will tell you things about yourself that even your friends won't.**

At some point in a trader's career, they may be able to adjust their trading rules based on their understanding of their historical psychological responses. But it usually takes years of experience in various market conditions to ensure these adjustments are logical, not emotional, ones.

For now, let's explore some of the main emotional pitfalls that traders—both new and experienced—often make, why they are detrimental to the trader, and what you should do if you encounter them.

BELIEVING YOU ARE SMARTER THAN THE MARKET

There are a number of emotional reactions that fall under the category of believing you are smarter than the market. Any time you start to trade based on what you think the market *should be* doing, instead of based on what the market *actually is* doing, you are travelling down a very dangerous path.

One of the greatest trading quotes I ever heard was from my mentor Bill Williams. Bill said, "want what the market wants." Any time you pick a fight with the market, you will not only lose, but you will be forever trading from a position of negativity. This will cause frustration, anger, hurt pride, and loss of capital.

So many traders feel that the market is out to get them, but they could not be further from the truth. They are out to get themselves, due to their mindset. They come to this conclusion because they have a hard time taking full responsibility for their trading results and will find any excuse to shift the blame for their lack of success.

They might claim that the market itself is out to get them by not doing what it is supposed to do based on their analysis, or that other traders are running their stops and taking them out just before the move happens.

The market moves based on the decisions of many traders. Messing with your specific position is not part of their goals.

Get over yourself, admit when you are wrong and accept the fact that not all trades will be profitable.

Whenever you're tempted to believe you're smarter than the market, remember (and apply) what Bill said: "want what the market wants."

THINKING IT'S THE MARKET'S MONEY

In this situation, you think you are playing with the market's money and not your own. If you make a profit on a trade, you think it is the market's money and so act like it doesn't matter if you lose it. Well, the truth is, that money is yours.

So many people tell me that they made X dollars on a trade and so they have more cushion on their next position, or their account is up X dollars so that means that they can afford to lose that much.

Guess what, if you have made a profit, that money is now yours and it should be protected just like your original capital. Why are you trading in the first place if not to make money and keep it?

It should not be difficult to convince people that money belongs to them, but for some reason it can be with trading. Just remember that trading is your business (you even have a detailed business plan to prove it), and the purpose of a business is to make money.

THINKING YOU KNOW AN INDUSTRY

Traders are often advised to choose instruments from an industry they are familiar with, since they may be more comfortable with it and have insights that the average trader lacks. This is often good advice. Of course, like most advice, there is also a risk involved in following it, and, in this case, you may feel you know how the market will react to information that you know to be true.

You may have a great handle on the fundamentals of an industry, but price action and fundamentals can often get out of sync. You may be very comfortable knowing that the industry as a whole and specific companies that you follow have experienced great success and will definitely see a period of increased revenues and earnings.

This bias will then creep into your trading and cause you to trade only from the long side, ignoring exit signals and short signals. These fundamentals may already be factored into the price, and your bias can cause significant losses.

Understand that the market doesn't value what you know in the same way that you do. Trade the market as it comes, not as you think it should be.

STAYING DOWN WHEN YOU FALL OFF THE HORSE

Losses, especially big ones, can have a huge impact on your ability to take your next trade. Losing dollars is one thing, but many also lose confidence—and confidence is a critical component to a trader's success.

The trick is simply to get back on the horse. Either taking a break or reducing size may help you to do this. (So, it's more about getting back on *any* horse—or even a pony—than about the exact same horse.)

Of course, you should evaluate *why* the big loss occurred in the first place and adjust your plan accordingly. This is often a good time to take a break and to re-evaluate why the losses have occurred. Does your system need tweaking, or did you break your rules?

However, this may just be part of a normal drawdown period, and the system you used signaled you to pull out of the market at the worst possible time, just as new trends were ready to be established.

Once you have taken the time to establish whether you made any mistakes, broke your own rules or the core trading rules, your system caused the losses, or you made emotional trades, it is usually better to get back on the horse and trade in some capacity than to stand aside. If you are scared to trade, this will help you to rebuild your confidence. If necessary, reduce your size, but try to stay in the game. The longer you avoid trading, the harder it may be to resume.

But if you truly feel that you are done trading, now is a good time to get out, as you have answered the first question posed in this book: "Is trading for me?"

Better late than never.

GIVING IT 'JUST ONE MORE DAY'

This emotional trap is commonly encountered by traders who have a long position on that has sold off, so it is now trading below the price at which they wanted to exit. They do not have a stop in place, wanting to manage their exits on their own.

Even though their trading rules say to exit, they intuit that there will be a bounce the next day and they will exit then instead. Do they sell? Of course not. Sure enough, the next day it continues to sell off.

Remember: a market that is oversold is just as likely to become *very* oversold as to bounce back.

In another example, you may have established a buy signal and see that the trigger price is hit, so your trading plan requires that you buy in. But you decide that, since the markets are currently overbought, the price is bound to come back down soon and you will be able to enter at a better price.

Of course, the next day the markets continue to move up and you want to kick yourself for the profits you should have been making.

This trap is easier to avoid if you have a robust trading plan in place and you regularly remind yourself not to deviate from that plan. Realistically, you are going to fall for this trap at some point anyway, but now that you know it *is* a trap, you might not fall for it more than once.

NOT BEING ABLE TO TAKE A LOSS

Some traders think that taking a loss on a trade is the same as admitting that they are losers. Their fragile egos can't allow this, so they will stubbornly hold on to a position until they prove that they are, in fact, winners. Sadly for them, this proof may never come.

At other times, a trader's position takes a large hit and the pain of taking the loss is so big that they become frozen, unable to make the decision to sell.

Trading is a business of buying and selling where the prices are highly variable and only partially predictable. Yes, you want to have some kind of edge that means you are right more often than you are wrong, but losing trades are an inevitable part of the business.

Losses should be taken quickly, analyzed, and then you should move on. I have heard stories of trading coaches who force their students to enter a position and then turn around and sell it at a loss immediately, just to familiarize themselves with the feeling.

Learning how to take a loss is an essential step along the trader's journey.

TRADING FOR THE THRILL OF IT

Let's face it, most people are initially drawn to trading for the money and the excitement. However, it is the combination of those two things that will kill you as a trader.

The only way to become a consistently profitable trader is to treat trading like a business. Of course, there are going to be times when you have a great run because you are in tune with the market; it was trending in your favor and your equity curve makes a nice move up. That will be very exciting.

Likewise, there will be choppy markets that inevitably will take back a piece of the equity curve and cause frustration.

The key is not to let these emotions influence your trading. If you want to chase a dopamine rush all the way to bankruptcy, head out to your local casino instead.

PERSONAL TRAUMA

Life happens, and during times of personal trauma, death, divorce, domestic issues, etc., it may be difficult to stay focused on your trading business.

You can persevere and try to trade through these emotional situations, but sometimes it is best to step away from trading until you are in a better physical and emotional state.

Controlling your trading behavior under normal conditions is challenging enough.

But what if trading itself becomes a source of trauma? Sometimes it is not your emotions that affect your trades, but your trades that affect your emotions.

Not sleeping at night, depression, and anxiety are just some indications that maybe you need to change the way you are trading.

Maybe your current positions are too risky, or you have just experienced a string of losses. Whatever it is, your body is telling you to either reduce your size or take a break. In some cases, it may be that the trading style you have chosen does not fit your personality, and in extreme cases trading may not be for you at all.

If you ignore these signals, ultimately it will impact your trading *and* your life. Humans will do some crazy things to avoid pain, and holding positions that have lost or are losing money can be *very* painful. I have seen people ignore their positions completely in order to avoid the pain of loss, as well as hiding brokerage statements from spouses and themselves.

Denial can be powerful, but acceptance and action are the only way to deal with these situations.

SUPERSTITIONS

I have seen some pretty weird trading behaviors driven by people's superstitions. It is one thing to wear your favorite socks or sweater when trading, that is harmless enough. But when your superstitions influence when or at what price you enter or exit a trade, this can become dangerous.

I have seen people wanting to buy or sell a stock only when it hits an exact price—even down to the specific cent value—that they consider a lucky number. They put in buy orders with the limit price set at the number they are attached to, and are often left with the order unfilled.

Looking for pennies can end up costing lots of dollars in missed opportunities.

BEING A PERMA-BEAR OR PERMA-BULL ONLY

Certain individuals just refuse to recognize that both bull and bear markets can and will exist, so they have a slant to one side of the market only.

Perennial bears in a bull market only see a top to short every time the market makes a new high. While perennial bulls believe every new low is a dip offering a bargain to be bought.

Of course, eventually they are both right, it's just that they usually have no capital left to trade with by the time their preferred conditions come around.

This is why it's so important to understand the market and its cycles—there are opportunities at all times.

FALLING IN LOVE WITH A STOCK

At some point, most successful companies eventually get a huge following in the market, initially by institutional investors and eventually by the public.

As more investors jump on board, the price moves up and is often followed by favorable fundamental news. Traders who participate in these moves often become blinded by the fact that what goes up must go down.

They ride the trend up, making more and more money as the price accelerates. These are the trades that everyone dreams about. Unfortunately, traders often fall in love with the stock and lose their objectivity. They believe the favorable action will continue and start to break their fundamental rules. "To the moon" and "Hold on for dear life" (often abbreviated to "HODL") are among the favorite slogans of these traders.

They continue to buy on dips and commit larger and larger percentages of their trading account to this one holding.

Of course, at some point, the party is over. Then, they end up not only losing all the profits they made on the way up but also losing considerably more capital than they expected.

Never fall in love with your stocks (or other trading instruments). They simply won't always love you back. Treat them like the fair-weather friends that they are.

BUYING TOPS AND SELLING BOTTOMS

Let's say you have been watching a stock for weeks. It has made new highs every day, and you are waiting for a pull back to jump on board. But the pullback just refuses to come.

Every day you say to yourself, "If only I had bought it when I first noticed it." You can't help but imagine all the profits that everyone except you are making. Finally, you give in and buy—at the exact time that everyone else starts taking profits.

CHAPTER 9

Or you buy a stock and decide you will use a mental stop at a price that soon your stock is trading at. It will bounce back, you think, and you set a new point at which point you will sell to break even.

Soon the stock is trading lower still, and you once again convince yourself that you will sell on the next bounce; a bounce that doesn't want to come.

The loss continues to mount, becoming more painful as each day passes. Finally, the stock seems to go into freefall—you cannot stand to hold for one more minute and sell at the exact time the bargain hunters enter the picture and drive the stock up.

As with so many emotional pitfalls, having and following a trading plan with rock-solid rules is key here. That, and adding automated stops to your trades.

TRYING TO BUY BOTTOMS OR SELLING TOPS

A rational person would assume that a stock can only rise so far before a sell-off and only go down so far before a rally.

Unfortunately, the markets are not rational, and prices can and often do overshoot any move that you may expect.

Many people are driven to be perfectionists and want to be the ones that pay the lowest price possible in down moves or short the highest price in a rally.

Remember that trying to pick the bottom is often referred to as "catching knives" for obvious reasons. It is best to wait for the markets to give an indication of a change in trend before attempting to enter.

FEAR OF MISSING OUT (FOMO)

Over-trading and lack of patience are two common problems that can have a devastating impact on your account.

Some traders just *need* to always have a position on. They are scared that the market will take off and they will have missed the best trade of their lives. I see this particularly with traders that are permanent bears. They think the markets are always on the edge of a major collapse and know that if they are not short the day the market finally sees what they see, they will miss out on making their fortune.

There are also traders who, although not necessarily looking for a catastrophic move, are expecting a trend to begin and do not want to miss it. They must have positions on all the time, and often their account is chopped to pieces during counter-trend moves or tumultuous market environments, where they should be standing aside.

No matter what happens in the market, there is usually plenty of time to get on even after a move has begun. Patience and a methodology that helps to identify the best times to enter are key.

BEING TOO STUBBORN TO GET OUT OF A LOSING POSITION

Many traders have a hard time admitting they are wrong.

They enter a trade expecting a profit and refuse to accept the fact that the move is going against them. For example, they will enter a trade based on a daily chart pattern and as the price hits the spot where they originally said they would exit, they look at the weekly chart and find a stop further away. I have seen extremes of this situation in which a trader is holding a portfolio of stocks all showing a loss from past years, waiting for the 'inevitable' return to breakeven.

I often joke that this is how traders with a losing position become investors.

Stubborn traders tend to become broke traders. If you don't work on developing your own sense of humility, the markets will do it for you.

BEING TOO EGO-DRIVEN TO STAY IN A WINNING POSITION

Although fear is a common emotion that triggers many bad trading behaviors, the *ego* is perhaps just as bad, making traders do some crazy things.

Cutting losses quickly is critical to any trading strategy, but not allowing a profit to move in your favor as much as possible before exiting the trade holds many traders back.

Once a trade is in a profitable situation—even if just above breakeven—many traders feel elated because they have been proven right in the trade so far. Fearing what little they have gained will be lost, and wanting the emotional high of the win, they often close the trade just before it really gets moving.

It might feel good to have a high win ratio, but increasing the average profits of your wins is where the money is. If your trading rules are sound, you can do this simply by following them to the letter.

FOCUSING ON PROFITS NOT PROCESS

Traders often get scared out of a great trade because they are focusing on the dollars involved and ignore their established exit plan. Often this is a sign that they are not comfortable with the size of the positions they have. They start to think of what they could buy with the dollars earned or at risk.

Increasing size is often a struggle. Instead of watching your profit and loss numbers, try focusing on your process and rules.

REVENGE TRADING

Trading is not a battle between you and a stock. Even if it were a battle, it would not be one that you should always expect to win. If you place a trade that does not work out, move on to the next opportunity with grace.

Follow your trading plan and re-enter if and only if it fits the parameters. A common emotional error is to re-enter a trade quickly in order to get back the money you just lost.

The need to be right, and the feeling that a particular stock owes you for the loss you just incurred, never ends well.

Learn to walk away.

LISTENING TO THE NEWS

Have you ever been watching the news online and seen a notification of a big move underway that you are not on? The temptation is to be part of the in-crowd and jump on board so you can say you participated.

Many traders like to brag about their gains and often fail to talk about their losses. They enjoy being able to tell their trading buddies that they were on the hot stock. Of course, by the time the move hits the news it is often over—you get in just when the profit-taking starts and you are left holding the bag.

"Buy the rumor, sell the news," is a Wall Street saying that reflects how prices and fundamental factors are related. It is also a successful rule of trading that is often ignored.

In fact, most traders do the exact opposite. One of the fundamental principles of technical analysis is that at any point in time, the price of a stock reflects all current and future fundamental factors. That would mean, for example, that if a company is believed to be growing and expected to have a good result (the rumor), then people would anticipate that and purchase the stock in advance of the news. When the positive news is released, and it could be something like positive earnings or a successful launch, then you often see that this is the end of a trend up, as professionals are selling into the news. Others hear the news and jump on board as prices start to fall.

Likewise, when the news is negative, the emotional traders sell at a price that has already reflected the event. This is a price that is normally a bargain, after others have panicked and sold their positions.

LISTENING TO TIPS OR RELYING ON OTHERS' ANALYSIS

One of the first tips most traders hear is "don't listen to tips." The second tip they hear is usually the one they trade.

One of the most important steps on the trader's journey is gaining the confidence to trade your own ideas. Traders can have a great strategy and trading plan but not follow it because they lack confidence, believing other traders know more than them.

This is understandable, especially when you are continuously bombarded by e-mails and social media posts proclaiming easy riches and strings of winning trades that defy logic.

The fact that most of these claims are bogus is one of the problems with following someone else's recommendations. You often only hear one side of the trade. You don't hear when to enter and the exit strategy that will determine its success or failure. The trading style may also be very different than what would be comfortable for you, or you may not even know what style they are recommending. The trade results may be theoretical, based on system-generated signals that were not actually traded, or in some cases just not true at all.

There is nothing wrong with gaining knowledge by studying other traders' methods and getting recommendations. I communicate regularly with a group of traders who share ideas. This is not the same as following trades blindly.

The key is to research the tip, see if it fits with your style and your rules, and decide whether you are comfortable with trading as the tip dictates.

TRYING TO TRADE LIKE SOMEONE ELSE

Show me ten successful traders and I will show you ten different trading styles. Each trader will have developed a style that matches their unique personality.

Traders, frustrated with their results, will often hear about another trader's success and try to emulate their style. It is also a problem with following anyone else's trade recommendations, whether from newsletters, blogs, or newspapers.

What you trade and how you trade must fit *you*.

CHANGING TRADING STYLES

Finding the right style for your personality is critical, and many traders will need to change styles a few times before they find one they are comfortable with.

That is fine, although the more time you spend studying trading and following the markets before you develop your trading plan, the better you will be at trading, right from the start.

Not giving your trading plan a chance, and continuously changing your style because of a loss, is an emotional response behavior and can be devastating to an account.

My advice is to enter the markets with a solid plan and confidence in your methodology. This will go a long way to preventing this behavior.

Be honest with yourself about whether it is the strategy, or your inability to trade it based on the rules, that needs improvement. If you are trading emotionally then that should be your area of focus.

TRADING INDICATORS INSTEAD OF PRICE

Some traders become obsessed with technical indicators, putting way too much faith in their predictive abilities. They forget that indicators themselves are derived from unpredictable variables—

price and volume—and like their names imply they are indicators, not predictors.

Indicators are great to help you see pricing through different lenses, but ultimately, they are only showing what *has happened*. Can they help put the odds in your favor? Sure, but they are only one tool of many—and it is *price* that you trade.

TRADING PENNY STOCKS (ASSUMING MORE RISK THAN YOU REALIZE)

Many new traders with limited capital are convinced that the only way to make significant money is to trade instruments that are volatile.

They compare large-cap stocks that maybe move 20% in a year to penny stocks that make the same moves daily. So of course, trading penny stocks is the way to go.

The underlying assumption is that they will be able to capture these moves, and there is the rub.

The risk involved and the emotional impact that trading pennies brings should not be ignored. As with everything else, understand the market and instruments you are trading, and ensure that they fit within your risk tolerance.

INCREASING YOUR POSITION SIZES AFTER PROFITABLE TRADES

There is nothing sweeter for a trader than a nice string of wins. Watching their equity curves rise, most traders can't help but get cocky.

You feel you are in tune with the market and start to think how much more money you would have made, if only you had bigger positions on. Your trading rules say you determine the position size by only risking 2% on any one trade, but is it really that big of a risk, if the markets are only moving one way?

So, for your next trade, you break the rules and put an all-or-nothing trade on. Guess what happens next? Your winning streak ends, and you give back most, if not all the gains you made.

Remember, markets only trend about 30% of the time, and, after a winning streak, most professionals *reduce* their position sizes, knowing that the end is near.

Confidence is great, overconfidence is not.

ADJUSTING YOUR STOPS BASED ON THE RESULTS OF YOUR LAST TRADE

The only thing worse than taking a large loss is taking a small loss and then having your stock turn around and make the move you were expecting, without you being on board.

You will kick yourself for the missed move and blame it on your stop or exit strategy. So, you adjust your methodology for your next trade, by giving yourself more room.

That stop gets hit as well, and you kick yourself for giving back more than you needed to. Then you adjust your stop again for the next trade, and so on and so on.

This behavior stems from both always wanting to be right and not having complete faith in your trading plan. Your plan should be tested, so that you have faith in the expected outcomes. The expected outcomes can only be expected if you follow the rules exactly.

Of course, you can re-evaluate the rules over time, but not after each and every trade.

COMMITTING TOO MUCH OR TOO LITTLE CAPITAL TO YOUR BUSINESS

The amount of capital you commit to trading has a huge impact on your ability to follow your trading plan. A small amount of capital often results in traders either taking on excessive risk to grow their account to a meaningful size or failing to take the business seriously because of the limited potential returns. Committing too much capital, on the other hand, often results in excessive fear, causing traders to make emotional decisions and deviate from their plan.

Balancing your strategy, risk profile, and capital commitment is a complex but important exercise that many traders overlook. Even when you find the right balance, as your account grows you must learn to adapt your strategy and your psychology along with it. Staying emotionally resilient is where consistent profitability lies.

TRADING NUANCES: WHEN TO ADJUST (OR BREAK) THE RULES

One of the things that makes trading so difficult is that for every reasonable rule that exists, there is a successful trader that breaks it.

Rules of thumb are great to protect new traders from risks, but once you become more proficient you can start to find opportunities outside of the safe zone. The road to trading success is a fine and continuously shifting line. Walking it is a balancing act. On the way there are few decisions with clear black and white choices, but there is a lot of grey.

For example, understanding and managing risk is one of the most important concepts to grasp and one that many new traders either do not appreciate or fully understand. Many jump in and assume excessive risks, so are quickly wiped out.

The key is to begin with a low-risk approach and establish money management rules to protect your capital. Once you have more experience you will begin to understand that there are times when more risk is appropriate and other times when you should be completely risk-off.

You also begin to see that the old adage that you need high risk to get high returns is not true. Finding low-risk trades with potential high returns is very much possible.

As traders begin to learn the business many inundate themselves by studying numerous approaches and analytical techniques. As we've established, it is important to gain knowledge, but many become overwhelmed and develop strategies that are overly complex, provide contradictory signals, and become impossible to trade.

A simpler, more focused approach is often where successful traders find their sweet spot.

As traders develop successful strategies, they come to feel that they are in control and that their analysis dictates outcomes, forgetting that they have absolutely no control over the market or price actions. They need to remind themselves to focus on what they can control: their process, trade execution, and emotional management.

Although trading with the trend is one of the cardinal rules, it is only possible when you know what the trend is. There are many traders who successfully counter trend trade. They focus on trend reversals and get on early to new trends, ignoring the current established trend that is ending.

Knowing when to shift gears is a skill.

There are certain character traits critical to a trader's success that often become problematic if not kept in check.

Traders need to be confident. Confident in themselves, their strategy, and their ability to execute their plans. It's when traders become overconfident that they run into problems.

Patience is another virtue that many traders have a hard time keeping in balance. Being too scared to enter a trade shows not patience, but fear. One that leads to missed opportunities. Not being patient enough and jumping into a trade before confirming that it conforms to your trading rules is greedy.

Many traders believe that the goal is to be able to trade with no emotions whatsoever. Just follow the rules that have an edge, and your success will be guaranteed. But traders are human, and as such have feelings, emotions, and thoughts that they cannot escape.

The real goal is to manage your reactions to these emotions, not to eliminate them. Through greater awareness of yourself, and the impact that these feelings, emotions, and thoughts have on your behavior, you can focus on the real goal: building mental resilience and taking control of your behavior.

Let's now look more closely at trader psychology, to better understand why these behaviors are happening and how to take control.

CHAPTER 10
TRADER PSYCHOLOGY II— LISTEN TO YOUR HEART AND TRADE WITH YOUR MIND

As you may have already guessed, I believe trading psychology is *the* most important element for traders to understand and deal with on their journey to success. Some will say it is money management that is most critical, while others will say it is your trading plan. In my mind, these are just the basic building blocks of any trader's approach. It is how you utilize those tools that is critical.

If you give ten traders the exact same trading plan, with specific trading and money management rules, I guarantee that you will end up with ten different results: probably from the very first trade. Why? Because no trader can operate without their emotions influencing how they follow the rules.

Unfortunately, as we have noted, the emotional reactions that traders experience are usually detrimental. This is the reason that nine out of ten traders fail. It is also something that must be looked at and addressed within yourself, with every trade you make.

When traders fail, they tend to fall back on tweaking the parameters of their system, hoping that will make a difference. This in itself is an emotional reaction. The trader is shifting the blame away from themselves, even though they know deep down that the fault lies within.

If you are struggling with trading, do yourself a favor and look over these emotional trading reactions, then go look in the mirror. Be honest with yourself and find out where you have been emotionally trading, and ask yourself again "is trading for me?" If it is, then recognize that by definition the business of trading is a high-stress endeavor. Your money is on the line, you have no control over the market, and the decisions *you* make determine your outcomes.

Your ability to handle the emotional impact that you are exposed to continuously—even with a successful trading plan—will ultimately determine whether you will succeed as a trader over the long term.

There are a number of ways to deal with the psychological side of trading. Some traders may feel that they are a waste of time or a little too flaky, but study and incorporate them, you will need their wisdom in the course of your trading career.

CHAPTER 10

BEING AWARE

The most important step in addressing your emotional responses is to be aware of what you are doing. Mindfulness is all the rage these days, and for good reason. Many people coast through life oblivious to what they are truly experiencing in the moment. When it comes to trading, you cannot afford that approach. Being mindful and aware of the cause of your behavior is a critical first step.

Before you place any trade, step back and ask yourself why you are doing it. Are you following your set of rules or are you caught up in the heat of the moment? The following set of steps will help you increase your awareness. By knowing what trading style is right for you, having a detailed trading plan, establishing and committing to your trading plan and the rules you created, and knowing what emotional triggers you may be predetermined to commit, you will have a disciplined approach that will help you to prevent the errors covered in the previous chapter.

Follow these steps in order:

1. Know what trading style is right for you.

2. Have a detailed trading plan documented. This will include specific rules for finding opportunities, entering a trade, exiting a trade, re-entering a trade, and the size of a trade.

3. Before a trade is placed, document why the trade is being placed, including a copy of the chart and how you are feeling at the time.

4. If you currently have trades on, review their current status against your trading plan to determine your current exit strategy. If you are a day trader this is being done throughout the day, otherwise review before the open.

5. When a position is closed, document the reason for the exit with a copy of the chart. Also review any re-entry opportunities against your trading plan rules.

6. Track all the trades you have made to capture at a minimum: date of entry, date of exit, quantity, entry price, and exit price. You can then calculate the length of time in the position and profit or loss. Cross-reference these entries with the documented individual trades.

7. Track your equity curve. Each day captures the total market value of all open positions, as well as any cash balance in your account. This represents your equity value. Tracking these values over time will provide you with your all-important equity curve. Viewing your equity curve is the fastest way to see how you are progressing as a trader. Ideally, you want to see a gently sloping upward curve, as you continue to build equity in your account. Of course, there will be drawdowns along the way, but you want these to be minimal, as you cut your losses short, when trades are unsuccessful.

As you can see, like the running of any business, I am suggesting a significant amount of tracking and documenting of your business activity. Of course, trading history and the accounting details will be available from your broker, so this part of tracking may seem redundant. However, the purpose of the tracking that I am suggesting is not so you can prepare your financial statements or tax returns. The main two purposes are to help prevent emotional trading and to form a solid foundation from which to learn. By analyzing the profit and loss statistics, you can identify which trades are most profitable for your style. This information is often surprising. Traders often have a favorite setup and think it is their bread and butter until they look closely at the results and are surprised to see that this is not the case.

Of course, by tracking, reviewing, and analyzing your trades and equity curve on a regular basis, you will gain many other insights that otherwise would remain lost to you. You also can see how your equity curve fluctuates with the various cycles of the market. Many traders initially focus on one cycle of the market only. For example, trading from the long side only. They will see the percentage of losses increase and their equity curves take a hit when markets are in a down-trend. In this case, they can then make adjustments to their trading plan to avoid these environments, or develop rules and strategies to profit during these down-trends, expanding their trading repertoire.

> **Only you are accountable for your trading results. Quit looking for excuses and take responsibility.**

This analysis and tracking is only a starting point to help you identify those areas where you are winning so you can continue and reinforce them, as well as identifying where you are struggling and losing so you can change your approach to avoid the same outcomes in the future.

Let's look at some of the approaches you can take to help address the emotional issues that are causing you to act against your best interest.

STAY IN SHAPE PHYSICALLY AND MENTALLY

Like any activity that requires your complete focus to keep you safe, trading is no exception. No one should trade when they are physically or mentally vulnerable, where their judgment is impaired. I know it has been a common theme, but one bad trade can set a trader back months, if not years, and it is critical that you are always aware of any situation that threatens your ability to follow the rules.

Exercising, keeping your weight under control, finding stress-reduction techniques, getting enough sleep, and eating a healthy diet are all key things that allow you to trade at your very best physical, mental, and emotional capacity. Traders need to maintain their basic physical and mental health. The usual recommendations for a healthy lifestyle apply as well. Eat right, find a physical activity you like, and get your weekly strength training and cardiovascular exercise.

Of course, life is not always that easy, and there will be times when you are experiencing stress or trauma over and above the usual day-to-day challenges. This will threaten your ability to trade effectively. The first step is to be aware of your emotional state. If you find yourself unable to focus, *stop* trading and deal with the issue immediately.

You may also find that, during trading, emotions will rise to the surface that may impair your decisions. The market is a great leveler. It is what it is, and no amount of hoping, praying, or begging will influence its behavior. This is very hard for intelligent, powerful, and otherwise successful individuals to handle. Many struggle with this truth, until they run out of capital. The sooner you are able to accept this fact and deal with the issues that come up, the better off you will be.

How to deal with these issues is different for each trader. Some find that the process of tracking their trades is enough. This is definitely a basic requirement and is a must for all traders. If you find that you still do not have the control you need, then you may need to investigate other options. Journal writing is very easy and is a powerful exercise that is recommended for many creative endeavors to help accelerate personal development. Journaling involves writing down your current thoughts to help clear your mind and develop your thought process. Do not discount this recommendation, as it is one of the most powerful and rewarding exercises that has huge benefits, not only to your trading skills, but to your overall personal growth. Most people think only on the surface. Journaling forces you to dig much deeper and get down to a subconscious level. You will find yourself solving complex problems, see things that were hidden from you before, and gain a much better handle on your trading processes, mindset, and emotions.

Meditation is also a great practice that will help you to handle stress and clear your mind. Meditation reduces stress hormones in the body, helps a person to stay calm in stressful situations, and improves focus. There are many ways to meditate, such as listening to music, doing guided meditations, focusing on being present as you enjoy your coffee or lunch and really focusing on the smells, tastes, and sounds of that experience. It can also be a walk in nature, where you admire the beauty around you and feel connected to the world.

Doing at least one meditative thing per day for as little as two minutes can help you to face trading challenges much better.

These are just a few suggestions for staying physically and mentally in shape. Of course, there are numerous other approaches that may fit your lifestyle better: massage, yoga, Pilates, weight training,

Tai Chi, Qigong, for example. The key is to commit to something and make it part of your plan.

IDENTIFYING YOUR LIMITING BELIEFS AND TURNING THEM INTO EMPOWERING BELIEFS

We trade our beliefs. Limiting beliefs will hold you back, resulting in losses, while empowering beliefs will propel you forward to consistent profitability.

Beliefs, of course, are only things we *believe* to be true. Many of our core beliefs have developed at a young age based on our personal experiences. Beliefs are often not based on any objective truth, but for us their impact is real.

It is amazing how much impact our beliefs have, not only on our trading, but on our lives. They have a huge impact on our behavior. It is also amazing how few individuals really identify and challenge their beliefs in order to improve themselves.

> **The market will keep teaching you the same lesson over and over until you either change your behavior, give up, or go broke.**

The good news is that beliefs can be changed. The first step is to dig deep and identify those beliefs that are negatively impacting our trading. Many of our beliefs help to guide our behaviors in very positive ways. However, when it comes to trading, many of the very fundamental beliefs that normally guide us to success have the opposite impact. There are other limiting beliefs that not only hurt our trading but other aspects of life.

Some of the common limiting beliefs that traders encounter are:

- Money doesn't grow on trees.
- The harder I work the more money I can make.
- I am not deserving of success.
- I am scared I will fail (or succeed).
- Trading is easy and big money can be made with little effort.
- The market and other traders are out to get me.

Empowering beliefs include:

- There are unlimited opportunities available.
- The money earned in trading is not based on how much time you commit but how effectively you use your time.
- I deserve to be a successful trader.
- I will commit to doing what is required to succeed.
- Success in trading required a strong commitment, hard work and effort to succeed.
- I am 100% responsible for my outcomes.

When it comes to our behavior, the impact from our beliefs becomes automatic. Like muscle memory, we just continue to lead our lives with little thought to why we do what we do.

After we have identified the negative beliefs, we can then more consciously observe our behaviors and start to connect the dots that show us why we do what we do. From there we can start to challenge the outcomes we are experiencing and position ourselves to make shifts for the better.

We begin by being aware of our feelings, emotions, and thoughts and what impact they have on our behavior. This is a practice that, once you commit to it, will amaze you with what you see. This is the real you, observing what you previously believed to be yourself. You will see the negative, limiting thoughts and self-talk you have been laboring under.

After observing, you will then be able to challenge the connections, replace limiting beliefs, and change self-talk from negative to positive. Continuous awareness and a conscious effort to change will result in your ability to behave in a way that supports your trading goals instead of sabotaging them.

You will find that this will not only impact your trading but also all other aspects of your life.

What I have described here is a major shift in awareness and will not be an easy exercise. In fact, it may require significant support in order to make the expected breakthroughs. I would start by studying the concepts and trying your best. I also encourage you to seek professional help as well as finding support with a trading group whose members are open to these concepts and willing to share and support each other through the changes.

Trading is a lonely business, and often we get stuck in a rut, unable to make progress. Finding a group with common experiences and objectives for improvement can make a big difference.

I believe that for many traders, the Holy Grail to success lies in this mindfulness area. You must learn to make trading decisions based on reflection rather than reaction. By changing your beliefs, being fully aware in the moment, and controlling your behavior—not letting your feelings, emotions, and thoughts drive your actions—you are on the right path to success.

CONCLUSION

THERE ARE MANY potential paths that a trader can take on their journey. Some paths are short and lead to failure. Traders who approach this business with visions of fast riches, requiring little effort on their part, are really gamblers—the markets will soon chew them up and spit them out. Others may put in some effort, but because the barriers to entry are so low, they jump in without the proper preparation and discipline required to achieve success.

Only traders who approach the business seriously have a realistic chance of success and long-term survival. This means dedicating years to the study of the markets and trading, and developing business and trading plans that they follow religiously and that evolve with the markets. They also realize that trading success is a mental exercise, rather than a fixed set of rules. They are continuously monitoring their own emotional state and have the discipline to stop themselves from trading outside the rules they have established.

This self-awareness is, in fact, one element of the Holy Grail that most traders are looking for. Unfortunately, many traders continue to look in the wrong place, amongst the vast range of different trading systems out there, instead of within.

> **The Holy Grail is to have a proven plan, the discipline to trade it consistently, the patience and will to stay the course through good times and bad and to let your equity compound over time.**

This book is meant to be a foundation of wisdom that you should become familiar with from the beginning of your trading journey. And so long as you remain a trader, you should continue to refer to it, to ensure you are not falling into the emotional pitfalls that can destroy a trading business.

I have outlined the key components of your education, business, and trading plan, but traders need to continually learn and evolve as the markets and technology change. Your trading practice and your plans must evolve too but be mindful of the delicate balance between keeping up and having so much knowledge that it can hurt you.

In my opinion, many traders spend way too much time, money, and energy on this aspect of the business. They are always looking for the next best thing and moving from one approach to another, instead of finding a few key approaches that they can specialize in and that fit their overall personalities. Many traders will have numerous indicators and trading rules, back tested and curve-fitted to their data, when a few simple rules would suffice. Even *with* their sophisticated rules, many traders still end up trading emotionally and experience poor results, far from what the system was designed to produce.

Trading is a business of probabilities, and one of those probabilities—the probability of success for those entering the business—is extremely low.

As the saying goes, "Many are called, but few are chosen." Many are called to trading by dreams of unlimited wealth and personal freedom. But only those who quickly realize that it is a serious business, and who discover a genuine passion and willingness to dedicate time and energy to learn and grow, are chosen. These few not only succeed financially, they also gain in personal strength and resilience, making them better people overall.

I hope this guide will help to put you on the right path, and I wish you all the best with your own personal *Trader's Journey*.

RECOMMENDED READING

OVER THE MANY years I have been involved in trading it has been amazing to observe the evolution of the material available to support traders. Before computers were on the scene, the primary resources were books. From a small number of classics when I began, we now have access to an almost unlimited quantity of written material. Once computers were available, the resources expanded to include software that now covers everything from charting, strategy design, back testing, and fundamental analysis to customized indicators and AI-based trading models.

It is mind boggling what is now available to support traders on their journey. There are many resources out there that I have not had any experience with so have not included.

Try not to let yourself get overwhelmed by what is available. Find a few good books to read about trading to help to determine the strategy that best aligns to your personality and goals. Once you determine your approach find the more detailed material to specialize in. Learn how to develop and test trading strategies and find software that supports this. Finally, find a broker whose platform supports your approach.

Like your trading strategy, the tools and material you use to support your business may change over time. Keep abreast of the latest developments and evolve as necessary.

For this section I am including the books that have had a big influence on me as a starting point for you.

CLASSICS

Here are a few classics written in the early 20th century by true pioneers in trading and investing who offer us timeless lessons:

- *How I Trade and Invest in Stocks and Bonds* by Richard Wyckoff, 1922

    Wyckoff was a pioneer in technical analysis, developing his Wyckoff method which outlines the key phases of the market cycle. In this book he also covers risk management and actionable strategies for trading and investing.

- *Reminiscences of a Stock Operator* by Edwin Lefèvre, 1923

    If there is one book that is on the shelves of the majority of traders, this is it. A classic published in 1923, it contains the timeless lessons traders need to know. The book is a fictionalized account of the life of the legendary trader Jesse Livermore. It is a story I go back to often that continues to entertain and inspire.

- *Security Analysis* by Benjamin Graham and David Dodd, 1934

    This is the bible for value investing, and the principles in it laid the foundation for Warren Buffett's approach (Warren was a student of Benjamin Graham at Columbia University). Although many technical traders want to ignore the fundamentals, Graham demonstrates that the more information you have, the better. This book offers a rigorous and disciplined approach to evaluating financial instruments.

- *The Wave Principle* by Ralph Nelson Elliott, 1938

    Elliott was another pioneer and developed a theory that market prices move in predictable recurring wave patterns driven by collective trader psychology. He also covers how Fibonacci numbers can be used to predict trends. I can imagine that there were many skeptics when this book came out, but many traders use the principles in their trading today.

- *How to Trade in Stocks* by Jesse Livermore, 1940

    Jesse Livermore is a trading legend who was one of Wall Street's most successful traders when this book was published. This is the trader whose life was fictionalized in *Reminiscences of a Stock Operator* on the previous page. This book is part history and part autobiography, but also covers details of Jesse's trading approach.

- *Technical Analysis of Stock Trends* by John Magee and Robert D. Edwards, 1948

    The bible of technical trading concepts that covers everything from chart patterns, trading tactics, stock selection, and money and risk management. This book has been continually updated with multiple new editions since its original publication. This really is the textbook for technical analysis.

- *45 Years in Wall Street* by William D. Gann, 1949

    W.D. Gann was a well-known trader whose methods many have been trying to understand for decades. He was very successful and often wrote in a very esoteric style that many believed was intentional to hide his true method of trading. In this book he does cover some practical rules and strategies for trading in stocks.

MODERN CLASSICS

Over time many new traders have built off the pioneering work from the classics, creating new theories and sharing their unique perspectives. Here are a few modern-day classics for your consideration:

- *How I Made $2,000,000 in the Stock Market: A Wall Street Classic* by Nicolas Darvas, 1960

  In this book Darvas, a world-famous dancer, shares his methods for trading in stocks that generated millions for him. He explains how he developed his trading method over time while travelling the world with no access to any of the modern tools. A classic foundational book for trend following.

- *Granville's New Key to Stock Market Profits* by Joseph Granville, 1963

  Although there are many market pundits these days, Granville was one of the first I recall becoming a famous market celebrity. Granville called for a market collapse based on his OBV (On Balance Volume) indicator and analysis. In his day he had a significant impact on daily moves in the market. At the time, using volume to help predict market turning points was an innovative theory.

- *Elliott Wave Principle: Key to Market Behavior* by Robert R. Prechter and A.J. Frost, 1978

  In this book the authors take the foundational theoretical work developed by Elliott and expand it into a more practical modernized guide for application by traders. It is still complex, but provides a more modern guide to wave analysis.

RECOMMENDED READING

- *How to Make Money in Stocks: A Winning System in Good Times or Bad* by William J. O'Neil, 1988

    This is the book I most often recommend to new stock traders. It is a classic guide that covers O'Neil's CANSLIM system for identifying winning growth stocks. It also covers detailed rules on entry, exits, stops, and risk management, so it is a great resource for building your trading plan. It contains lots of great charts and continues to receive new editions long after its original publication.

- *Stan Weinstein's Secrets For Profiting in Bull and Bear Markets* by Stan Weinstein, 1988

    There are many theories on how markets move within cycles over time, and I believe the topic is foundational to trading. In this book, Weinstein covers his methods to recognize and trade the various stages in his four-stage cycle model. Another powerful foundation to build off of.

- *Market Wizards: Interviews with Top Traders* by Jack D. Schwager, 1989

    With literally an infinite number of ways to trade, one of the best places to start is by reviewing other traders' methods, successes, and secrets. Jack has written many books in the Market Wizards series, which every new trader should review before diving into any one trading style. Alignment is critical and this is a great place to start. This series is another one of my most recommended reads.

- *Trading for a Living: Psychology, Trading Tactics, Money Management* by Alexander Elder, 1993

    Dr. Elder was another big influence on me. He, like Bill Williams, was a trained psychologist. As psychology is a major component of traders' success, it is great to see new authors with this focus. This book not only covers trader psychology but also includes all aspects of a trading plan, including the innovative 'Triple Screen Trading System.'

- *Trading Chaos: Applying Expert Techniques to Maximize Your Profits* by Bill M. Williams, 1995

    This is the one book that really resonated with me when I first read it. It covers Bill's application of chaos theory to the financial markets with a very detailed strategy as well as a unique approach to trader psychology that sparked my interest in further studies. I was lucky enough to have been able to study with Bill, and he had a major influence on how I trade and view the markets.

- *Trade Your Way to Financial Freedom* by Van K. Tharp, 1998

    Van K. Tharp was another very popular writer and trading coach. This book is a comprehensive guide on how to build a trading system that you are aligned with. He covers a number of critical aspects that many overlook, including position sizing and expectancy.

- *Technical Analysis of the Financial Markets: A Comprehensive Guide to Trading Methods and Applications* by John J. Murphy, 1999

    This is another great guide that covers a large number of technical analysis topics and trading essentials—a great resource for building your own trading plan.

- *The Encyclopedia of Chart Patterns* by Thomas Bulkowski, 2000

    When developing your strategic edge, it is great to know what works and what doesn't when it comes to traditional chart patterns. In this case Bulkowski has done the rigorous testing and analysis and provided it in this book for your reference.

RECOMMENDED READING

- *Trading in the Zone: Master the Market with Confidence, Discipline, and a Winning Attitude* by Mark Douglas, 2000

  If you ask a trader who their go-to is for market psychology, Mark Douglas is the name they are likely to mention. This book focuses on mastering the trader mindset. It also covers the five key truths traders need to embrace to attain a probability mindset: anything can happen, you don't need to predict markets, wins and losses are random, an edge is just higher probability, and every trade is unique.

- *Technical Analysis: Power Tools for Active Investors* by Gerald Appel, 2005

  As a fan of the MACD indicator myself, I am including this book by Gerald Appel, who developed the indicator. He presents many strategies and techniques suitable for multiple timeframes.

- *The Daily Trading Coach: 101 Lessons for Becoming Your Own Trading Psychologist* by Brett N. Steenbarger, 2009

  Brett Steenbarger has been many traders' go-to trading coach. In this book he presents an approach for traders to coach themselves, with numerous lessons, challenges, and assignments to help you achieve trading success.

- *Trade Like a Stock Market Wizard: How to Achieve Super Performance in Stocks in Any Market* by Mark Minervini, 2013

  Mark Minervini is one of the original Market Wizards interviewed by Jack Schwager in his series. A successful trader who is a dedicated mentor and coach to many, in this book he reveals his own system, which includes everything from stock selection to risk management. This is a great book to leverage techniques from a trader with a long-term proven track record.

I can honestly say that my trading library includes well over 100 titles, so this is just a small sample of what is available for you to read. Whatever books you decide to pick up, I hope you enjoy them as much as I have and that they contribute to your learning and success.

ACKNOWLEDGMENTS

Although trading may be a solidary endeavor, the journey of learning to trade—and writing and publishing a book about it—is anything but.

I would first like to thank the numerous brokers who took my curiosity seriously when I was a teenager with an interest in the stock market, and who shared the experiences and knowledge that laid a solid foundation for me to build from.

I also acknowledge the numerous authors who have filled my library and brain with new ideas and stories to entertain and challenge in the ever-evolving trading landscape.

I am deeply grateful to the professional traders who have literally opened their doors and mentored me.

To my trading partners over the years for your ongoing collaboration and shared successes.

To the camaraderie, shared knowledge, and friendships that have grown from joining and attending investment clubs and meetups, where special bonds that only traders can understand and appreciate develop.

To the engaging and supportive community of Twitter/X where I began my social media adventures, sharing my experiences and learning from fellow traders.

Being a published author has always been a dream of mine, and my sincere thanks to Harriman House for giving me the opportunity to share my lessons with you all. Thank you to Nick and Craig for the amazing editing and collaboration to make this a reality.

Lastly, thank you to my family, friends, and colleagues for listening to my tales, encouraging me, and giving me the confidence to write my book.

ABOUT THE AUTHOR

Peter Robbins is a highly experienced trader with over 50 years of navigating the markets. His extensive career spans corporate finance and investments in the medical technology and insurance industries, as well as serving as a corporate controller in the building industry. Throughout his journey, trading has always been his passion. Whether full-time or part-time, he has always made time to trade.

Peter's trading style has evolved over the years, from day trading futures, swing trading stocks and options, to position trading ETFs. He is dedicated to sharing his knowledge and insights, mentoring fellow traders, and fostering a sense of community. With an online presence of over 100,000 followers, Peter regularly shares the wisdom he has gleaned from a lifetime of trading—empowering others on their paths to success.